Dear Chris,
Always
yourself & embrace
changing woman.
Namaste
Sincerely,
Sandra

Early Acclaim for Journey with Daisy: Belonging is a Blessing

"I was impressed with the strength, courage and determination of both Sandra and Daisy. They were two women (one in her 60's and one in her 90's) who met at a crossroads in both of their lives. In the epilogue, Sandra explains that the story has been about tests of endurance – the endurance of not only Sandra and Daisy but also, Daisy's clients, the developmentally challenged adults who steal your heart in the story. When I read about the fear, anger, pain, questions, healing, transformation, bliss, power, and freedom inherent in their intersecting journeys, I felt that my own journey as a 'budding Crone' had been honored as well."

Patricia Stockwell, B.Ed. M.Ed. English and Counseling Psychology.

"The author has written about a difficult stage in her life when a major source of inspiration and mentoring was a 91 year-old woman named Daisy. Sandra brings Daisy's "Treasure Trove" to life and learns many lessons as she meets its many and sometimes frequent visitors. It is an enjoyable and absorbing account of her ongoing experiences as an authentic and spiritual human being. I recommend it for all of us who are dedicated to personal growth especially, women."

Dr. Marion Reed, BA. MDCM., FRCP (C). Psychiatrist in private practice.

"A Journey with Daisy: Belonging is a Blessing" is a challenging and rewarding read telling Daisy's story of kindness, courage and tenacity. Daisy is a very special ninety-plus woman who brings to mind our own close elder women friends. Cleverly intertwining her experiences with Daisy's, Sandra takes inspiration from Daisy to keep striving on her own personal journey. Hers is a journey filed with bumps in the road."

Sandra Davis, BA. Teacher-Librarian (retired)

"A Journey with Daisy: Belonging is a Blessing" is a testimonial to the author's inner strength and resilience. It was reflected back by Daisy and her people that surrounded her and held her safe. I appreciate Sandra's willingness to be so open and raw. Who would know that when Sandra was in search of her people, she was really in search for her authentic self?"

Lynne Edel, Holistic Practitioner.

"I want to thank Sandra for writing this story and for her well articulated expressions of self. By allowing her vulnerability to show, she has succeeded in relaying some very strong messages that many could benefit from reading. I must say, that there were several parts that I could personally relate to and I am not too proud to say that many tears filled my eyes. I appreciate how much her story stirred strong emotion, as I believe, true change, requires it."

Gordon Hayne, Youth counselor, Family Support Worker, and Foster Parent.

"I wish to thank Sandra for sharing so much of her heart and that of Daisy's in "A Journey with Daisy; Belonging is a Blessing." I know that the traditional response is that, "I couldn't put it down." Well, I did have to put it down many times because I found myself working through issues that surfaced as I read through Sandra's experiences at the Treasure Trove. It took time and tears and what felt like a lot of emotional work and introspection to be able to arrive at the last page of the book but the impact was enormous. Sandra has allowed me to leap forward in terms of my own personal growth with a greater understanding of my own and the greater female struggles that span our lifetimes."

Jan Marquez, MA. Tourism Planning.

"I thoroughly enjoyed reading "A Journey with Daisy: Belonging is a Blessing." It is a wonderful mix of reality, compassion, and psychology."

Adriana Lankoff, BA. Minister of Metaphysics.

"I found the content of "A Journey with Daisy: Belonging is a Blessing" to be fascinating. It was difficult for me to put it down and when I did, I hurried whatever I was doing to get back to find out what was happening next.

It was intriguing to realize the connection between the author, Sandra, and Daisy. One thing that became very clear to me is how much Daisy truly cared for those who were less fortunate and she gave of her self many times over. The Modern Services for the Handicapped has provided many opportunities for people to get to know one another as well as to get to know themselves.

I wish to thank Sandra Johnston, the author, for coming into my mother's life when she did. Not only has the writing of this book meant a lot to my mom; it has created stronger feelings in me for my mother and her commitment all of these years to those less fortunate. Daisy helped Sandra to find her way and in return, Sandra shared her journey by writing this book.

It is my hope that the contents of this book will provide the readers with a journey that will open their hearts to others who need just a few minutes of time."

Wendie Davidson, B.Ed. M.Ed. Educational Consultant.

Daisy's Daughter.

"I got the same calm feelings from the book as I did when I read 'Eat, Pray and Love'."

Trina Frank, Dental Hygienist

"This is the story of an inspirational woman whose 'Little Shop of Healing' made a difference in the world."

Colleen Ryan MBA.

Other Books by Sandra C. Johnston:

In Her Own Time: A Woman's Journey to Self

*Tracking the Predator: The Aftermath of September 11th, 2001
...A Canadian Woman Speaks*

Sandra is working on her next books:

Extraordinarily Ordinary
and
Of Cats and Other Tales

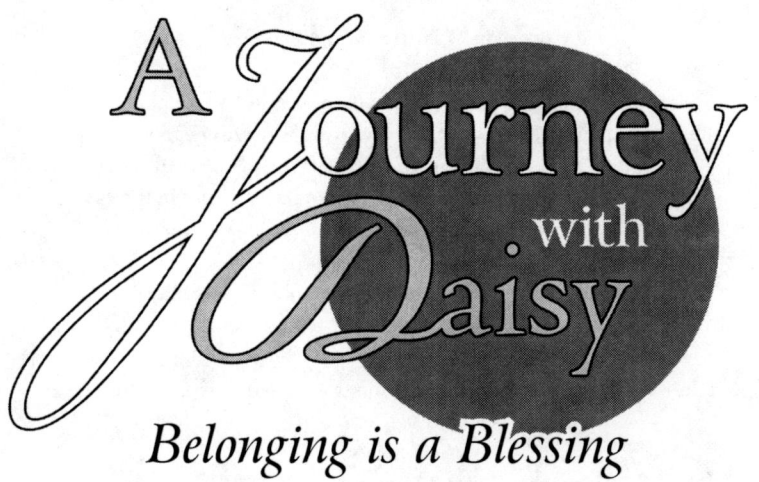

A Journey with Daisy

Belonging is a Blessing

Sandra C. Johnston

iUniverse, Inc.
Bloomington

A Journey with Daisy
Belonging is a Blessing

Copyright © 2010 Sandra C. Johnston

All rights reserved. No part of this book may be used or reproduced by any means, graphic, electronic, or mechanical, including photocopying, recording, taping or by any information storage retrieval system without the written permission of the publisher except in the case of brief quotations embodied in critical articles and reviews.

To protect the identities of those involved in this story, some of the names have been changed.

iUniverse books may be ordered through booksellers or by contacting:

iUniverse
1663 Liberty Drive
Bloomington, IN 47403
www.iuniverse.com
1-800-Authors (1-800-288-4677)

Because of the dynamic nature of the Internet, any Web addresses or links contained in this book may have changed since publication and may no longer be valid. The views expressed in this work are solely those of the author and do not necessarily reflect the views of the publisher, and the publisher hereby disclaims any responsibility for them.

ISBN: 978-1-4502-7178-3 (pbk)
ISBN: 978-1-4502-7179-0 (cloth)
ISBN: 978-1-4502-7180-6 (ebk)

Printed in the United States of America

iUniverse rev. date: 11/20/2010

"I am a therapist on the page. I try to care for souls as I write about the soul."

Thomas Moore: "A Life at Work."

Author's Dedication

I dedicate "A Journey with Daisy: Belonging is a Blessing" to Daisy Walls, Jessie O'Neill, and Anne Griffith. Jessie and Anne were my first spiritual mothers and my sacred time with them in Ontario prepared me for my travels with Daisy.

These 'elder' women gave me life, courage and a deeper faith. I treasure the fact that we have been women together, that we have sat in circles together. I have been nourished, empowered, and loved unconditionally in their presence, as well as inspired to continue to peer behind the veils of illusion with the hooded eyes of an owl.

These three wise women helped me to find myself and to define who I wanted to become. The lessons that they taught me will come out throughout this entire book, particularly the parts that reference the need for role models, a nourishing support system and reverence for our feminine fierceness as well as our generosity.

I hope that these experiences, words, and ideas inspire you with new thoughts, old memories and warm feelings.

Writing this book has been one of the most fulfilling joys of my life in spite of the obstacles. It has reminded me of how happy and proud I am to be a woman. I understand at a very deep level the courage that it takes to heal in our culture at this time in this era. Writing is a form of ritual for me in terms of putting my life into perspective. It called forth the shades and specters in my life and has helped me put them to rest. It speaks to evidence of past hardships, courage and triumph over adversity. I have been a survivor in terms of past injury. It is the admiring of it now, rather than the being of it, that will release me. To realize injury and memorialize it allows thriving to come into form. Thriving is what is meant for us on this earth and not just surviving is our birthright.

For centuries, being different has meant standing at the edge, and one is practically guaranteed to make an original contribution to the culture.

I have been labeled defiant, rebellious, a troublemaker, unruly, too smart for my own britches, noisy; but all along, I believe I have been on the right track.

The riches of my life are abundant as I come to know more deeply and appreciate my womanliness. I am Maiden, Mother and Crone. I am the changer and the changed.

May this book inspire you to have an open heart and to remember who you are at your very core - A Child of the Universe!

Daisy's Dedication

I dedicate this book to my daughters: Patricia, Wendie, and Deanna. I wish love and peace to all the readers of this book.

Acknowledgements

This book is for all my relations great and small.

I wish to thank and bless my daughter, Tara Johnston-Lee for her support and diligence by helping me with the manuscript technically, but most of all for the safe place and love that she granted me while I processed much of the material for the book. I offer thanks to her husband, Donald Lee who supported Tara in her love for me. I wish to honor the little dogs, Willow and Brodie who accompanied me on my long walks in Banff, and my cat, Simba who gave me solace as he sat beside me when I wrote. I wish to thank Daisy Walls for her presence and love in my life and all of 'her people' who taught me so much about life, compassion, and loving. I am very grateful to Ann Westlake, my editor, who gave me guidance and female nutritional support as well as exercising her excellent editing skills. I am grateful for Linda Carreno's sensitivity and creativity in terms of her input regarding the cover images and the web design.

Preface

Meeting at the Crossroads

When I moved to White Rock, British Columbia, I had it in mind to continue my work as a psychotherapist and movement therapist. I came with a 'herstory' of forty years of teaching and counseling experience. I was drawn to the western shores of the Pacific Ocean because I felt depleted from caretaking in my practice, as well as on the home front, and I was losing vitality. I knew that this would be an act of courage, and I did fear that it might be difficult to make a career change in my sixties, especially in a new province. I sensed that there was something important about this new place and I knew that it would not all be good.

I started to practice at a healing facility in April, 2009, and then received news of my father's passing in mid-May and had to return to Ontario for his funeral. When I arrived back, I was very ill with bronchitis and was forced to take what I thought would be a short-term sabbatical.

Truth has a way of finding us when we least expect it, and my body was having the last word. I had taught what I needed most to learn. I was completely out of energy and I knew, at some level, that I was not ready to resume any kind of energy work with others. I did know that I had some soul work to complete and it would require several ingredients: naked honesty, stamina, tenderness, sweetness, ventilation of rage and humor. This medicine would help me to call my soul home.

In the meantime, I amused myself with hunting for thrift store treasures and writing. I did not put great faith in my writing, even though I had already published two books on psycho - spiritual development. I did not have the financial resources to market them. I was continually at odds with a complex inside of me that was formed by words and perceptions of others around me, that writing was a luxury and was a 'pie in the sky' idea. I had taken faulty advice hook line and 'sink her'! Daisy's Treasure Trove in White Rock, was one of the thrift stores that I frequented. I felt drawn to go there every week because I liked Daisy and I loved hunting for treasures. Over time, even though all I had to live on was a small disability pension, I asked her if I could volunteer to help her and she was delighted.

I was slotted in to work at Daisy's Treasure Trove on Wednesdays with another volunteer, and on Saturdays with Daisy. Every day became a rich experience for me in terms of meeting, listening and watching people. Something became useful in all the torque and tension. I was being tempered and made stronger.

I mentioned to Daisy over time that I would really be interested in writing her story and logging my experiences in shorter stories. She was pleased with the idea. So, this book is written in praise of Daisy Walls, a ninety-one year old woman, who I was fortunate to meet at another crossroads of my life. Not only did I want to write the story, I also wanted to live it and so the everyday stories and my life evolved as well.

I hope that this book will serve to deepen you, make you smile, become more compassionate and more seasoned just as I was through Daisy's story and the experiences that I share with you.

Read, weep, enjoy, grow and laugh out loud!

Introduction

The Wise Women of Age

The Crone is the old wise woman that dwells as energy in all women, along with the energies of the Maiden and Mother. These energies are associated with the moon-tides every month but unfortunately, most of us have not been taught the importance of the monthly flow in time. The moon-tides do run in our blood at all times and this is an important concept in terms of honoring the feminine energies.

We recognize the Maiden Energy at the time of the new moon and remember the vitality of the girl that dwells in us. The Mother Energy is represented by the full moon and reminds us of our fertility and capacity for nurturance. It is a time when we must nurture ourselves so that we can sustain the energy to nurture others. The Dark Moon represents the time at the end of the monthly cycle when introversion and self-analysis is required. It is a time for re-grouping and knowing what is enough in terms of energy expended. This is Crone Energy.

These natural rhythms are within us at all times: Maiden, Mother and Crone. When we notice a young girl skipping down the street with a smile on her face, full of energy and potential, we witness Maiden Energy. When she stops to pet and nurture a kitten, we see Mother Energy, and when she speaks clearly with pearls of wisdom, she is in her Crone aspect.

The trouble with the socialization process for girls and women is that we have been encouraged to over-identify with Mother Energy. This makes us 'good' women of the culture but also leads to becoming dry- boned and wizened over time. Developing a respect for the old woman or Crone Energy in us helps us to know and keep our boundaries so that we can appropriately limit our Mother Energy and preserve our vitality, the Maiden Energy.

The fact that we lost Princess Diana and Mother Teresa the same year created a deeply unconscious mourning all over the world because of the loss of the Maiden and the Crone. Were we all losing hope without awareness of the wounding that was taking place?

I was at a crossroads in my life when I met Daisy. I do have a faith that everything happens for greater reasons than we can comprehend at the time. I have studied enough feminine psychology to know that the function of women of age who hold the blood and the wisdom is to assist people who are no longer where they were and not yet hope to go. This was exactly where I found myself in White Rock, formulating this question: Is Daisy a mid wife to something that was about to be constellated in me? Was this an emergency situation when something was about to arise spontaneously from the depth of my unconscious – a song, a spirit, a new being emerging?

I have had the privilege of working over the years with older women in my practice as a psychotherapist. I hold a great respect for them as I am now learning to have for myself. It has become a personal mandate for me to rail against the imposed redundancy of older women that has been extant in our culture for way too long. The task is, and has been formidable, in a politic constantly being handed down that carries residuals of bloodied massacres of wise elder women during the Inquisitions. From my own personal experience and the experiences of many women whom I have heard into speech, I believe that we are still experiencing a clandestine inquisition of women who dare to rail against the status quo.

The Crone represents a stage of life in which wisdom is sought – a time of introversion and spiritual seeking. It is an active exploration into the dark terrain of the unknown self where we search for the lost Maiden, the vital self, the feminine source of life. Basically, the Crone represents the menopausal phase of a woman's life, when she can begin to think very seriously of spiritual meaning, and embark on a quest that had previously been out of reach to her when she was engaged in the usual female function of childbearing and child rearing. I was entering that Crone period in my life once more when I met Daisy. I needed to turn to inner questions and incubate away from the world for a while. This, of course, needs to happen every month for girls and women menstruating. The Crone, or Dark Moon phase that occurs when the uterus sloughs off, requires a time away from the world – to rest, to reflect, to journal, to daydream and get to know oneself. It is usually labeled a pre-menstrual symptom problem and one is medicated in order to be kept in the world without creating problems. Herein lays the hostility problem for girls and women that presents as a danger to the many that do not give credence to the moon cycles and their relevance to our blood times. How sad! Menopausal women are also medicated and perceived as depressed, ornery, nasty ambivalent nuisances that heat up. This is the time when a woman begins holding the blood, a metaphor for the holding of acquired wisdom. It is a time for a woman to move more deeply into herself so that she can begin to relate to herself and others in a more authentic manner… She now signifies a turning away from the external social space of people, and parties in favor of the inner darker realm of the unconscious psyche. She becomes a pilgrim, of sorts, now radiating humility and inner strength. The Crone aspect of a woman keeps her inner fires burning so that she can feel her vitality and maintain her child-likeness along with her wisdom. The Crone, or Wise Woman, has learned the power of holding energy and transmutation, and she chooses how to spend her energies. Her libido sinks into her own depths. She represents a 'time out' from relationships and turning inward that will rejuvenate. My time has come again. In this withdrawing, we are able to find a way out just as a caterpillar weaves its cocoon before it emerges as a beautiful butterfly. Part of the process of weaving a future for us depends on being able to divine what lies ahead, as well as making sense out of the past.

There was a time in history when women were diminished in the eyes of men because of religious and political reasons for 'power over' as defined by Patriarchy. The medial powers of older wise women were repressed and came out in twisted and tortured forms of witchcraft and sorcery. Thus, we have arrived at a place where women's power within is seen as frightening and as a needing to be witch-like. This was a terrible denigration to women of age and personal power. The ability to go into the unconscious and come back out again is a necessary vital part of any soul's search for meaning, which is what the power of the Crone or medial woman represents. Out of our dark wait and expectation comes the birth moment…of creativity, song, poetry, story, or prophesy…always a breakthrough and not a breaking down. The energy now moves her into insight.

The Crone represents authentic power, ability to heal and to project healing power onto others. I have been a witness to this many times in my experience with older women. Now, Daisy inspires me to write and speak the truth as I have come to know it. The older woman in her full Crone aspect has earned her healing powers. Turning away from the world to discover whether you are really alive can be very painful. It means an acceptance of loneliness…when there is nothing to do… the natural power of healing occurs.

I have nothing to do now…only to experience and write. Each day at Daisy's takes me deeper inwards and this is a part of the spiritual journey that one sometimes cannot share even with the most like-minded.

I am that woman, right now, who represents the loner or separatist who is paring down all that is alienating against my natural flow and confining away from my natural Self. This is a prying away of layers of the false self from the true Self, finding who one is at the core of one's being. Encasing the Self is the core of all authentic separation or individuation.

Women in Patriarchy desperately need to engage in 'creative boundary living' in order to escape from the prevalence of victimization and enter into a new landscape of personal integrity. We seek transformation, and change is the only constant. We have only to observe Mother Nature to confirm this. She has blown fierce at times to clean up. When we spin the cocoon and go inward, we later emerge as something new. We learn to sense our own position and motion.

I am a woman now in deep process, watching Daisy as she navigates the world and communes with those who come into her presence. I am learning delicate balance. The distance I have to travel now is to the homeland of my Self. I hope that through the listening and watching that I will become more intuitive, a teacher and 'way-shower' to others. As Daisy lives each day, I see her make her knowledge visible and she demands respect. Her store, her network, is a paradigm of creativity and those who fear her will not enter her space.

The Crone or Wise Woman of age is whole unto herself…and an example to us as to what it means to be more than female, more than male. Her active inner self shines out to touch others with the wisdom and knowledge she gains on her journey. 'Unweaving' deceptions and illusions in my own life are preparing me to sink more deeply into my personal power and virtues. I am naming my truth as I have come to know it.

I look forward to this task…this weaving and recasting of all that I have learned.

Eventually, I may re-emerge into the world once more, but for now, I have decided to retreat into myself and to volunteer at Daisy's…awaiting the joyous energies and restoration of my Self in her presence. She is a gift to me. Thank you, Daisy!

1

"Look, then, into thine heart and write!"
Henry Wadsworth Longfellow

When a writer decides to tell a story, the teller never knows the outcome. This is the magic of the story.

Stories set our inner lives into motion when they might be frightened, wedged or cornered. They can point to a way out a way out. May these stories about my experiences at Daisy's Treasure Trove lead you back to your real life. May these tales bring you insight, encourage you to live passionately, give you the breath to speak what you know, deliver nourishing soul food, and inspire you with the courage to face what you see without looking away from it.

This is a book of telling about my personal experience with an 'elder' woman. I met her on my path of re-discovery of my essential Self. To diagram her, to draw boxes around her life would be contrary to her spirit and mine. To have come to know her was to know more about myself, an ongoing process. I am sure that it will be lifelong work for me even after I complete the story.

So, here are some stories that you can use as food for your soul, some observations and some fragments that can serve to help you map new psychic territory.

Here is to true life!

It all began on an unseasonably warm day, in April, in White Rock, British Columbia. I had committed to help my new bosses paint their healing center before the grand opening but I did not have enough cash to cover the cost of the required parking time metered on the available parking lots. I had passed by Daisy's Treasure Trove a few times, always with the intention of stopping into the store to browse. Thrift shops have intrigued me ever since my grandmother called me with such joy to her bedroom after she had visited the local bargain store. It seemed to me then, that she had to hide her treasures from Grandpa, but she delighted in showing her bargains to me behind closed doors. Perhaps it was her way of sneaking a little life for herself.

I parked in front of the Treasure Trove and entered the store. A gentle-faced lady stylishly dressed with carefully coiffed white hair and remarkable blue-gray eyes greeted me.

"I have a problem," I was honest with her.

"Tell me your problem," she smiled at me.

"Are you Daisy?" I wanted to know.

"Yes, I am, and how can I help you?" she continued to query.

"I need a parking space for the day because I am helping people to paint their store and I realize that I don't have enough money for the parking meters. I was wondering what you might charge for the day. I have five dollars with me."

Daisy wrote a note on a heart shaped piece of paper letting the meter man know that her space had been paid for and she instructed me to place the notice on my dashboard. I was so relieved because the real truth was that five dollars was all the money I had for the next week. My trip west had been a financial drain. I was full of hope, however.

"Thank you so much, Daisy, and I promise to be back to see you." I left to fulfill my obligations.

A few weeks later, after the painting of the healing center had been completed, I went to visit with Daisy and to see her treasures. She was interested in me and inquired, "What line of work are you in?"

I had a conversation with her then about coming to the west

coast, landing in White Rock, and intending to resume my work as a psychotherapist, movement therapist and educator. She asked me to bring her some business cards and told me that she would be happy to send business my way but that she would like to know more about me. I learned that day that she created the store originally to help the handicapped and the challenged people in the area and that it was registered in Victoria as Modern Services for the Handicapped. In the moments that I was engaged with Daisy in conversation, I became aware of the presence of two people in the store who continued to ask her about their next duties and she directed them. I was well aware by the time I left the premises that they could not seem to initiate store activities on their own and relied upon Daisy for defined instructions regarding their responsibilities.

Daisy Irene Jansen was incarnated into the world on September fifteenth, 1918 in Czar, Alberta. She was the fourth born of eight children in this order: Mary, Ruby, Gertrude, Daisy, Helen, Evelyn, Archie and a brother Gordon who had passed away in infancy. Daisy's mother, Lydia Lillian Schafer, was born in Turner, Iowa. Her father, Gordon Edwin Jansen had been born in Russia.

Daisy remembers her mother sharing with her that her father, "was one of the good lookers at school with wavy hair." She told Daisy that of all of the girls, "I won him over." "He did not turn out to be the prize package that my mother thought he was, but he was good to us kids." I was aware that this was the child's assessment of her mother's unhappiness and her own ambivalence toward her father.

I was curious and asked how her father showed love for her mother.

"I did not see love because I knew that he liked the ladies. He was a charmer. I never saw my parents hug or kiss," she revealed.

"What do you remember most about your mother, Daisy?"

"Well, I believe that mother was a good wife having baby after baby," she answered and then added," I don't remember mother without a swollen belly ever." Daisy, engaged in deep thought, then went on. "We moved a lot as a family all over the prairies it seemed. My father was a farmer and I went to a lot of different schools."

"Was that difficult for you, Daisy?" I felt compassionate for the child in her.

"No, I don't believe that it was hard. I guess that I thought it was kind of special and I did not know any better," she reframed the dynamics of her childhood.

"It must have been difficult to make friends," I commented.

"I was just so homely," she stated seriously. I could not help but giggle because I had never heard anyone say that about oneself.

I remarked feeing stunned by the revelation, "Really Daisy?"

"I don't think that the kids liked to play with me. My hair was shaped like a bowl, except that the sides were longer and I had bangs. I wasn't up with the styles of the times and I wore hand-me-down clothes," she smiled at me. Here I was sitting in a thrift shop surrounded by second-hand clothes!

I started to feel sad as I sat beside this beautiful woman and I began to wonder how different she might have felt when she compared herself to others. I felt as though I had a soul connection to her.

Rick, who lived behind the store entered at that point and asked Daisy about the size of the tutu she had in the window. She started to laugh and replied, "I don't think that it will fit you, Rick."

"I am just teasing you Daisy. I do need a costume for a Halloween party, and I know for sure that I need a black tie." Daisy got up from her chair and went to get a bag from behind the store counter.

"Rick, hold on. I have a gift for you." She must have sensed his anxiety. Rick looked surprised and Daisy asked me to grab the camera off the shelf and to take a picture of the two of them as Rick opened the gift. He lifted up an orange shirt that she had bought especially for him to wear for Halloween. She informed him that she had purchased it at Wal-Mart the previous evening. I snapped a picture of them together.

Rick became creative. "I saw an orange mask in the window, too. I think that it would look good if I wore it on the top of my head." He went to get it from the window and Daisy just smiled. We all started to laugh when he donned the mask and it looked as though it had built in ear muffs with the face of the mask sitting in the top of his head. This was a wonderful 'funny bone' moment; I had not experienced one like that in a long time.

I moved to the clothing room to find a black tie and found one that was indigo blue. We all agreed that it served the purpose. Rick looked absolutely hilarious when he added the tie to his repertoire. We were child-like in our mirth: two women together who were accessing their Maiden energies and Parsifal, the bumbling knight in search of the Holy Grail!

A woman entered the store at that point and smiled at the antics. She went on to browse within earshot of us.

"Rick, there are some grass skirts in there." Daisy pointed to the Halloween section in the clothing room. I went in to help him find one. "I don't think it will go around your bottom." I grinned at him. The grass on the skirt just covered the front of his body and his hips when he tied it on. The customer was giggling now and made a suggestion that he might consider wearing a pair of tights.

"But then his bottom would be sticking out!" I was bent over laughing and I know that all present had the same visual image because we are all screaming with full belly laughter. Rick decided to get serious, "I think that I will go to Wal-Mart to find some tights but I will bring over a coffee for you, Sandra, and a hot chocolate for you, Daisy, before I go," and he left.

The customer found what she was looking for, but I am not sure that it was only the clothing that she coveted now. It is amazing what community and laughter can do to lift our spirits.

This was a wonderful ritual to have experienced in the season of 'All Hallows'.

I got back to the interview that I had started earlier with Daisy when Rick returned with the promised libations, and a pumpkin that he intended to carve for Daisy's front window.

"What kind of face would you like me to carve, Daisy?"

"An Oriental one," she stated seriously.

"I will try," Rick conceded and exited once again in search of tights! He promised to return on the holiday or might I say, the 'holy day' of Halloween.

I still had a few moments with Daisy alone. "Tell me about your first good friend, Daisy."

"Well," she went on, "I never really had one until my late forties when I came to White Rock. I met a woman who was recovering from a nervous breakdown. She told me that she kept having children and felt out of control of her life. She also told me that she felt like she couldn't get up from going under."

Reminded of what Daisy had shared earlier with me about her mother and her own experience, I was surprised to hear her speak of the loneliness. Presently, and in the short time that I have been gifted by her presence, so many people who love her surrounded her.

"Tell me about your earliest memory of your childhood," I continued to query.

She began, "I remember having to put on fleece lined bloomers and long socks everyday." Daisy pointed to her feet. "And these long black boots with many buttons that I had to lace with a hook. Can you imagine a little child's hands having to do that? That was all that we knew though, and we had to get used to it." She generalized and I felt tremendous compassion for the little girl in her again.

Daisy went on, "I remember my mother going over to a house that we could see from the windows of our house. The lady there was having a baby and Mother was acting as a mid-wife. She told us that if a baby was born before we went to bed that she would set out a white flag. We never really got to know when the baby was born." I sensed her disappointment.

"I can also remember having to travel everywhere by sleigh and horses all covered up in blankets filled with horsehair. I was the only one, or so it seemed to me then, who continued to worry about where we were going to pee. Mother always told me that I would just have to hold it." I was aware of the empathic failure.

I was surprised when she reiterated, "You know, I never remember my parents having hugs and kisses. You just did not do that in those days. So, I made sure that I gave my children lots of them."

I felt a deep sadness then for the many mothers, including myself, who unconsciously gave out of the well of their own unmet needs. Didn't a lot of us seem to get used to it? Was I looking to Daisy even now to consciously mother me with her deep wisdom gathered from personal experiences? Had she experienced being exiled like me? Don't all women unconsciously long to be mothered by a conscious mother that we can stay identified with? Did I also need to share my revelations with Daisy, still feeling the void in me left from my past and my own experience with a collapsed mother? I was untaught at a most basic level. It is a mother who teaches her children what to watch out for, what to pay attention to, those things that are not known to them until the mother shows them, thereby activating new learning and deep wisdom from within. My instincts had never been sharpened, and I was left with distrust of my own perceptions.

As I spent time with Daisy, I realized that I could identify with her at so many levels. Perhaps my decision to write her story was divinely guided by my imminent Creator. I vowed to stay open to the mystery.

Daisy began again after a short reverie, "You know Sandra, I wanted to be a dancer but I was told that dancing was a sin and that was that! I got into doing some tap dancing on my own with those big boots that I had so much trouble tying." I became aware of her ability to sustain her passion in spite of the invective.

I recovered a memory then that I shared with Daisy. "I also had a deep passion to tap dance, Daisy. I had met a friend when I was ten years old at a camp. She lived twelve miles away from the small town where I lived. We made a strong friendship at camp and stayed connected by phone. She knew about my longing to dance and her mother gave her permission to sell me her old tap shoes. I was so determined to get them that I saved up my allowance for weeks and dealt with a local bus company to arrange to pick them up at the local travel agency. My parents never found out about the purchase because I put them in my backpack and took them to school with me. It was not that I was forbidden to dance; it was that I was always being told that I had crazy ideas.

I was so proud and excited! I put the shoes on at the entranceway to the school and clickety-cliked down the hallway until the principal reprimanded me and demanded that I remove them. I felt shamed then. I hid the shoes and I never tap danced again.

I wonder now how that might have been the beginning of my tendency to have a secret life and to feel as though I had to 'sneak a life'. My writing has been dissident. I seemed for a very long time to need so much permission to do what was most exciting and creative for me. I felt the sadness and tears trickled down toward my mouth. I licked the brine on my lips.

I had met a man while I was in White Rock and moved in with him. I was very vulnerable financially, and my former roommate and I had to go in our separate directions. He offered to help me to get grounded and told me that he was very aware that I needed to rest. He did not like that I was at Daisy's on a volunteer basis nor did he like that I felt compelled to write this story. Even now as I sit writing, he is coming down the hallway from the bedroom. It is after twelve o'clock in the evening. He shames me, "What are you doing out here, having another party?" I am continuing to write without saying a word. He is headed back to bed.

I am retrieving an image of my mother sitting in the living room eating ice cream and watching television alone. My sisters and I were in bed. My father would come out of the bedroom and say the very same thing to her. She obviously was enjoying the silence of the night *just as I was. Did she feel guilty and shamed? I never got to know my mother well enough to understand the workings of her soul. I would have to guess.*

As we were getting ready to close the store for the day, I asked Daisy to save the little hand drum that was behind the counter. I told her that drumming was good for the arthritis in my hands and that I could drum to my favorite music. She said, "Sure, but then you will have to come and play for us!"

"Well Daisy," I replied, "I don't consider myself a drummer but I can drum!" I laughed out loud. I became aware then that this is what creativity and passion is really about. If one wants to dance, then dance; if one wants to sing, then sing; if one wants to be loved, then love; if one wants to write, then write, and the beat can go on!

Daisy offered me a story then. "I remember going to Whitehorse on a holiday once and I consider that to have been a very important event in my life. I was there for just a short time and I met an old native woman who chewed deerskin to make Muck-lucks. She seemed to me to be a very sad woman. She told me that the priests came to the reserve and took her children away to Residential School. She explained to me that she had never had the opportunity to know her grandchildren, especially her granddaughter. She lamented the fact that she would never have the opportunity to teach her the native language, to do beadwork or to chew the deerskin. I was so taken by this native woman that I went everyday from the Lodge where I was staying to her house. I wanted to know about her life. The day that I was to leave, I walked over to her house to say, good-bye." Daisy's eyes started to water and she spoke through the tears, "She held me tightly in her arms and whispered into my ear that she was giving me a pair of Muck-lucks. We stood for a long while and cried together. I really felt the love flowing between us."

"You experienced some very holy moments with her, Daisy, and you were connected through your sad but tender hearts," I responded.

Daisy caught my eyes then and said, "You know, Sandra, I don't think that I am a very spiritual woman yet."

At that moment I felt the tears coming and I spoke through them, "Oh Daisy, I feel the Divine in you so clearly in my heart and I am grateful that I have the privilege of being in your presence. I feel fully present with you, just as you were with the native woman."

Just as Daisy went to visit the native woman everyday when she was in Whitehorse, I found myself wanting to visit Daisy everyday that I was in White Rock. I was warmed by Daisy's story.

I had worked for three native reserves in the field of psychotherapy for several years. Listening to so much pain and loss that the native people suffered at the hands of the white man made my heart hurt. I believe that, like Daisy, my own deep compassion and identification with them had to do with an awareness operating at a deep level. I had suffered subordination like so many women, some men, children, and minority groups in this culture. I was also indoctrinated by a religion that taught me that the institution had my best interests at heart. That was not my personal experience at any level of my awareness.

When I was a child, I saved my allowance for the Missions in poor countries. I made an exception for the tap shoes. I could never consider at such an innocent young age that a melt down of some of the Ecclesiastical chalices in Rome could feed those third world countries! Putting money and energy into the coffers of institutions that offered redemption from intrinsic evil was all part of the early brainwashing that made captives of so many children. I wished that I could feel more blessed than I did and perhaps I would not have succumbed to the addiction to approval that made me a captured woman most of my life.

I now believe that Crone wisdom is not about keeping secrets, nor is it about any interest in maintaining the status quo, especially the emphasis on capitalistic economy.

2

> "Good writing is a kind of skating which carries the performer off to where he would not go."
>
> *Ralph Waldo Emerson*

It was a rainy Saturday in October and I whipped open my umbrella to make my way to Daisy's store. I wondered what this new day would bring and how the events of the day would unfold.

Daisy was standing up straight behind the counter when I arrived and asked me how I was feeling. I had been down with influenza earlier in the week. I felt much better just entering her space and being with her.

Daisy was happy that I put a tote hanger on the wall on Wednesday. "Put price tags on the mittens, hats, and scarves that go into the tote. I'd like you to put tags on the front of the tote pockets too. That way the customers will know what are in the slots," she directed me. I moved to fulfill her wishes one by one when Neva, who was assisting that day, came to the back of the store with a handful of scarves that had just arrived. We were working in close proximity to one another. I really enjoyed working with Neva because she was efficient and we laughed a lot.

A customer rooting through a basket that was sitting next to Daisy's chair, she held up a black rain hat and exclaimed, "I wish that I had this hat this morning!"

Luva Lynne was tending to her Guatemalan wares of jewelry, hats, scarves, key chains, worry dolls, and other artifacts. She overheard heard her and shared a personal memory with the woman. "I remember my father used a part of my mother's nylon stocking to wear on his head to keep his hair straight while it dried, and he would often wear one under his whaling hat on certain days."

This was the first time I knew that the kind of hat that was a find for this lady was called a 'whaling' hat. The customer exclaimed, "My father used to do that too! I am so happy to hear that someone else did that!" She laughed out loud and everyone within earshot joined in.

Johnny, who worked for Daisy two days a week, came into the store shortly after and exclaimed in front of all of us, "I need to find some exercise wear!" I had noticed that Daisy took special interest in Johnny. He had a speech problem, but he was strong, competent and helpful to her. He did not seem as wounded as were some of the others under her counsel. He usually appeared as though he has just rolled out of bed leaving his hair disheveled and sporting whatever clothes were easily accessible,

He started to rummage around me while I was pricing things for the tote. He let out a sigh and brought out a white outfit that consisted of a jacket and pants to show me. "You look like you are a Karate student, Johnny," I commented.

"No, Sandra, I am going to start my own exercise program in my living room and I need to wear something that is comfortable," he stated seriously. The happy young man entered the dressing room and then exited proudly. "Do you think these pants are too short?" He modeled them for me.

Neva came back with a few more scarves to hang up and heard Johnny's question to me, "You just need to let the hem down some," she observed.

"My mother can do that for me because she started to take sewing lessons," he smiled. The ecstatic grin on Johnny's face was enough to melt any heart. He was so happy to share his treasures with Daisy now and he offered her his price. Daisy accepted his offering and made sure that he took his apple for the day with him when he left.

She looked at me after his exit and added, "Johnny needs that apple because he does not get enough fruit to eat at the lodge where he lives."

Luva Lynne was in the process of sorting and displaying her Guatemalan earrings. She showed Daisy a pair that was meant to help arthritis sufferers. Daisy beckoned me to come over to where they stood.

"Look at these earrings that Luva Lynne has. She said that her mother wore these types for her arthritis and they helped her; you might consider getting a pair." She added, "You might want to put more oil into your body. I take a teaspoon a day with a piece of toast to make it more palatable." Daisy moved to her chair and asked me to sit beside her. She took my right hand in her hands and began to show me how to massage warm olive oil into them. "I do this every evening without fail. You should wear gloves and wear them all night." How could I second-guess this prescription when I looked into her bright eyes and felt her stroke my fingers and hands with her warm pliant fingers and hands that show no signs of crippling?

"You know, Sandra, I lift two pound weights every night because they help to keep my muscles taut." Daisy flexed her biceps to demonstrate and once again I was inspired to do the same.

Another customer entered at the same time that she was rubbing my hand. "This is Louise, Sandra," Daisy introduced us. "She drives for 'Driving Miss Daisy'." I was very curious now and opened a conversation with Louise.

"Tell me exactly what it is that you do?"

"I drive seniors to their destinations and stay with them until they are finished with their appointments." I wanted to know more when another customer came into the store to pay for the treasures that she had laid away a few days earlier.

"Everyone seems to know you, Daisy!" she observed with a smile.

"Well they should," Daisy retorted. "I have been in business in White Rock for thirty- seven years." Her face lit up and she smiled broadly at the customer. My curiosity was piqued even more.

Another customer squeaked through the little crowd that had gathered at the entranceway and wanted to know if Daisy had a potato shredder. "Up the stairs and to the right," Daisy directed. She located one, paid for it and left.

I asked Louise to tell me more about her business. "I have elderly parents and I knew first hand that there was a need for this kind of service. I have always wanted to help people beyond what was allowed in a regular job and I wanted to have fun as well. I hoped that I could do something that would involve assisting the senior population so they did not feel so alone and marginalized. I wanted to be someone that they could count on and help them feel important in this society. I accompany them to their appointments when they feel worried and nervous and I wait for them until they are finished. I also have the privilege of driving special needs children; I get to experience how very special they are and how their parents cope. I have learned a great deal of compassion and something new everyday. I appreciate my clients and I have fun. It is wonderful that I can drive Daisy to work when she needs transportation and I get to say that I drive Miss Daisy!"

I was warmed and impressed by this young woman who stood in front of me articulating clearly that she had found her vocation. I witnessed her as being one of our cultural creatives who found a genuine need in the community, and who decided to give from her heart space. Louise left and the store was quiet. Daisy asked Luva Lynne, Neva, and me to come and sit with her for an 'apple break'. Luva Lynne had brought us freshly picked apples from a neighbor's tree. Daisy directed Neva to bring the children's Halloween costumes with her when she came to sit. She wanted them displayed in the front of the store and we sorted them while we took the break. " So many of the children's Halloween costumes nowadays are ready-made and the young ones are losing out on the imaginative experiences of putting things together to wear," she lamented.

I recalled and shared with the women the joy that I had of searching through closets at home, at my grandmother's house, and my friends' houses for 'dress up garbs'. The creativity and anticipation was as much fun as getting treats.

I felt the need to do some more sorting after our break. There was a big basket sitting beside Daisy's chair and I asked her whether she wanted me to go through it. "Leave it for the customers to sort through and find treasures," she answered. I recognized right then that she was into practicing what she was preaching.

Another day ended at Daisy's and Rick walked in the door to ask if there was anything he could do to help us close the store. Daisy asked him to move some of the things that were outside on the walkway back into the store and to put out the garbage.

Daisy explained to me, "Rick does this quite often and I truly appreciate his help. He lost his wife to cancer earlier in the year and he is in the 'between time'."

I believe that we are all in the between time in this October season. Halloween is a liminal time according to the old cultures. It has been said that ancestral spirits walk close to the earth and that we possess a heightened ability to access the unconscious and bring that knowledge to the topside world.

Luva Lynne remarked when I shared this knowledge, "I have been in many metaphysical stores over the years as seller and buyer, and it is my experience that Daisy's store holds more energy than many."

What I have come to know is that I have found a place where I feel safe, a place for discourse and not debate, a place where I can speak up in order to feel some personal power, and a place where I feel respected and valued.

Daisy's Treasure Trove is a thrift store and she is a woman who has gathered in a wealth and range of experiences. She has held them *within her until they percolated into wisdom. I was grateful this day that I could take my full place at her table. I honor her and I want to be like her. I want to be a responsible steward on this Earth walk and a model of mature feminine development.*

3

"Happiness comes from the capacity to feel deeply, to enjoy simply, to think freely, to be needed, and to risk life."

Storm Jameson

Daisy called me to come into the store on Tuesday in order to prepare me for my shift on Wednesday afternoon. While I was there, she received a phone call from Rosalea, who comes in to dust and clean for her on Wednesdays. She asked Daisy to put a brown blouse with a tie on it aside for her that she had seen the last time she was at the store. Daisy directed me to search for and hang it in a special section that was like a lay-away for special customers.

When I went to work on Wednesday, a lady was standing outside of the store door with her little dog. "I did not know that this store existed," she greeted me with a smile. "I am dog sitting down the road and I live in Cloverdale," she spoke, while she followed me into the store.

"Just take your time," I offered.

Rosalea arrived a few minutes later and introduced herself to me. "I am here to clean," she explained and scurried off with her dust rags and a Windex bottle.

An elderly gentleman wearing a quality brown suit and tie came into the store and headed for the men's section. He came out to show me some brown shoes that he discovered, so I directed him to a chair because he needed to try them on. "These are excellent shoes, but I fear that they may be a tad too big." They were just as he thought they would be and he moved to return them to the shoe shelf.

The lady with the dog found a dress and a blouse and she wanted me to show her some jewelry. I opened the door to the chest and she directed me to bring out certain pieces that she could see more clearly. She sighted a pair of oversized pearl and gold earrings and asked if she could look into a mirror. I located the mirror and she modeled them for me.

"I really like these, but I would have to find someplace special to wear them."

"Everyday is special," I said and she smiled while she admired herself in the looking glass.

"I grew my hair long again," she primped. I had a strong sense that this woman was into retrieval of some part of her that she had lost or repressed. She continued, "I read somewhere that geologists found remnants of jewelry from the cave man period." I added that I also knew that historically, or might I say, 'herstorically' that women used to grind stones into powder to color their faces and lips. "Self decoration is a creative province of the feminine and how or whether one chooses to decorate oneself is a personal language, conveying whatever a woman wishes."

"Obviously, this ritual is about honoring the feminine," she smiled broadly. She looked at some more pieces, selected those that she felt were within her budget and asked me to tally up the items.

"Can I pay with my debit card?" she queried. I had to tell her that we took cash only. She asked me to hold the items while she went to the bank machine up the street and I assured her that they would be there when she returned.

The elderly gentleman asked me for a shoehorn. Being new to the job, I looked for Rosalea, and she directed me to the wall beside the shoe rack. This man was delighted, "I have found a pair of shoes in decent shape that fit me like a glove!" They cost him $2.50 and he happily counted his change for me. He thanked me for the great deal and off he went. I recognized how delighted I was feeling observing people feeling happy about their treasures. It was a far cry from sitting in a chair all day listening to pain. I was not getting paid, but I was finding out more about what felt rewarding for me. This was my task at this stage of my life. I knew at some level that I had to hang on tightly to my resolve to retrieve some of those parts of me that were underground. I needed a guide, the scent, and the trail that would lead me home to my authentic self. Another woman had arrived in the store after the shoe payment and asked me to show her the beaded dress that was hanging on the wall in the clothing room. "I would like to make a skirt out of it," she explained. I was not sure how to get it down off the wall so I found a broom to assist me. She was delighted and headed for the change room with a cache of other items.

Johnny came on the scene for his daily apple and feeling of connection. I was relieved because I had some questions about operations that I needed him to answer. I knew that he had been in the store for a long time, and he liked the responsibility of teaching me. I focused on a box of hangers that needed unraveling after he left. There were a few things in a garbage bag that had been left at the door the night before that needed sorting and hanging. That is part of the daily ritual at Daisy's and it takes time and patience.

The 'dress lady' beamed when she exited the dressing room. "Everything fits, I can't believe it!" she exclaimed. She also wanted to look at some jewelry and purchased a couple of very unique items from Daisy's treasure chest. "I used to be a designer," she quipped when I commented on how creatively she was dressed. "I love looking at thrift shops because they stimulate my creativity because of the unique items one might find." She paid me and left the store a very satisfied woman.

Rosalea who had been hard at work asked me to write a note to Daisy to remind her that she was almost out of Windex. "How long have you been working here, Sandra?" she asked in her very meek voice.

"I have been working here for just a few days, Rosalea." I responded.

"And now you are a store manager?"

"No, not really, Rosalea. I just enjoy people and I have always loved to shop in thrift stores and hunt for treasures."

"I have known Daisy a long time and she has lived a very rich life," she commented.

"I would like to write a book about her and perhaps you can help me over time when you are here." I was almost pleading, hoping that someone who had been close to Daisy could help me to put the story together.

"I would be happy to assist you," she offered, as she got ready to leave for the day. She had left every little nick knack and the shelves that displayed them spotless. "Women like treasure hunting and getting a bargain," she added. I was aware of the pride that Rosalea demonstrated in doing her tasks and I was relieved by her willingness to help me.

The lady with the dog returned to pay for her things after finding the bank machine. "I have no dog now, so I have some more time to browse."

"Go right ahead and enjoy yourself," I encouraged her.

It was close to closing time, but I knew from my own experience how wonderful it is for a woman to have time to browse and dream. This fine woman told me that she had raised a handicapped daughter with very little financial support, and that she had also volunteered at a thrift shop that subsidized the handicapped.

We had a connection now as the girl/maiden in this woman came to life in Daisy's store that day. She was not feeling any pressure and she had the time to look at the pretty and unusual things. I could not help but remember that time when that was all that I needed to keep centered and inspired. Some have called it retail therapy, but I have come to know that it is much more than that. Sometimes I enter a flower shop for the same reasons. I just stand there and let the scent of the flowers fill me.

I locked the door and while I walked home, I mused that I had spent a good part of my life accepting poor bargains. In the now, I was into treasure hunting and treasuring blessed moments in time. I was finding sacredness in the ordinary. I hesitated to go into my apartment because I was not sure that I had not made a poor bargain once again in terms of my decision to live with a man who had offered to help me when I was very vulnerable. I had lived alone for a long time before coming to the west coast. I needed some relief and I was suffering from financial strain. I did know for sure that being with Daisy and greeting the customers helped me to maintain my sanity while I was sorting out this issue.

4

"Art is the stored honey of the human soul,
gathered on the wings of misery and travail."

Theodore Dreiser

It was a Saturday in October at Daisy's Treasure Trove. Daisy had opened the store before I arrived and a gentleman wearing a baseball hat, a western shirt, and suspenders that held his baggy pants entered along with me. Daisy introduced him as Ernie and I could tell by their greeting that they had known one another for a long time. Ernie had just returned to White Rock from his cabin at Jones Lake.

"I have been in the hospital for four days with breathing problems because the air was thin up there."

"Have you been taking good care of yourself?" Daisy questioned him and offered him an apple.

"I can't chew'em because I have no teeth," he lamented.

"Well, you should shred them and put a bit of sugar on'em because they are so good for you."

"I was wondering if you have any belts." Ernie tried to change the subject. I offered to look in the men's wear section and Daisy started to root through the belts in the front of the store.

I found a couple of men's belts for him to try but they were not big enough. Daisy came up short in the front section. She did try to get him to try on a lady's belt but it did not fit either.

"Do you have any shirts with snap buttons?" He pointed

to the snap closures on the shirt that he was wearing. I went to the men's section again to find the special shirt but had no luck finding one of those either.

"I'm originally from Alberta and there's more Western flare there. I just thought I would get lucky here."

"I'll keep my eyes open for one," I offered.

Ernie stood up then and said, "I saw a picture of myself recently from when I was in my twenties. I had all of my teeth and a full head of hair. I couldn't believe that it was me."

Daisy interrupted his thought process and said, "You can't go there again so just stop that talk."

"No, that's the truth, but I am happy that I gave up smoking, or I wouldn't be here," he responded proudly shifting his belt to bring up his pants.

"Was that difficult for you?" I asked him.

"No, not when the doctors told me that I'd be carrying a breathing machine on my chest," he put his hand on his heart area.

Ernie was about to take his leave and told Daisy that he would be back to get a belt. I sensed that he thoroughly enjoyed his visit and the banter with Daisy. I was glad to have met him and I looked forward to his next visit. I hoped that a belt and a snap button shirt of his liking would come into the store soon.

A sprightly looking woman wearing a bright orange sweat suit entered next. She was looking for a picture of a girl that she had seen in the store earlier in the week. I remember when two pictures had come in together in a bag and I had set them near the front window. One was of a girl and the other of a boy. I wondered why someone would donate family portraits, and who would purchase them.

"It is too bad that you did not buy it when you were in when it was priced at twenty dollars." Daisy sounded admonishing. "I have learned since then that the pictures were painted by a well-known artist and were worth a hundred dollars each."

"Drats," the lady said. "I wanted that for my dining room but

I did not know whether it would suit the area until I went home. It just goes to show you that when something appeals to you, one should get it." She began to browse some more. I watched her over time and was aware that this lady had a familiar energy about her and I had to ask her whether we had met before.

"No, but everyone tells me that I have a regular face and resemble Judy Dench. I am not sure if that is a compliment, or not." She laughed heartily.

I could not help myself from trying to figure out how I might have known her because there was something that endeared me to her. She left and then it dawned on me I had participated in some girls' dancing last New Year's Eve just after I moved to White Rock. We had a wonderful time as we laughed and talked a great deal that evening, and she told me that it would be fun to have me as a friend. I felt it too. I wished that I could have remembered the incident and shared it with her.

Another woman then entered the store with a look of hostility on her face. She said something that I thought was very inappropriate to Daisy. "You can be a whacko, Daisy," she said with a sardonic grin.

I immediately stated, "Daisy is one of the wisest people I know."

I had seen Daisy's face blanch and I could sense that she was resonating from the remark that was not called for. After the woman left I sat beside Daisy for a short break and Daisy disclosed to me right away that she felt hurt by the remark. "That woman is full of it in here," Daisy pointed to her heart."

"You mean hostility, Daisy," I said, and she nodded affirmatively.

"You know, Daisy," I offered some soothing, "That is what is called a projection on her part. What I mean by that is that some people try to deflect onto others parts of themselves that they are unable to integrate within themselves. As long as they can find someone to be a willing container for them, they can energetically dump their shadow on to the other at that person's expense. In other words, she feels like a whacko at times and has not dealt with her own thoughts about herself."

Daisy nodded that she understood and said, "I will not contain that energy or let it affect me."

"Good for you, Daisy, because you don't want to end up feeling her fear and insecurity." I also knew that this awareness was a major aspect of my own healing journey.

I was always amazed at Daisy's perspicacity! Once she became aware of something she meant business. I knew that she would respond differently the next time someone projected onto her and be able to maintain her vital energy. Was I tapping into Crone wisdom? Most certainly I was!

Next, a young man in his early twenties came through the door and greeted Daisy with a big smile. He bought an I-pod the size of a quarter and asked Daisy, "Any new watches come in, Daisy?"

Daisy introduced me to Bill. "He is a collector of all kinds of watches, Sandra, and he is here because I wanted him to appraise some of the watches that I had kept at home. She turned to Bill. "I haven't got them here today, Bill, but I promise to have them next week." She picked up a hat from a bag next to her that had just come into the store. "This looks like it would suit you, Bill," she offered.

Bill put the cap on and he was ecstatic. "It is just what I need, Daisy, to round out my Halloween costume! How did you know?"

Daisy smiled at him and winked at me. "I'll be back to see you next week, Daisy, and thanks for the hat." He bounced out the door.

Rick came in next with a cup of coffee for me and a hot chocolate for Daisy. He seemed to sense that we needed a break. He left and Daisy and I took a pause to refresh. I had been sorting another bag of goodies and had found some pajama pants that I thought might look good on Daisy. I lifted them to show her.

"I only wear pretty white nightgowns, and that is a gift that I give myself," Daisy responded.

I retrieved a memory then of a faded old blue housecoat that I wore when my children were growing up. I never gave any thought to night finery or pretty under garments. It is only recently that I have understood the importance of treating me to things that made me feel nourished. I was learning to put myself into the equation so to speak. With my father's passing in May, care taking days ended in the sense that I was choosing when to give care and becoming much more selective in terms of energy input and output.

That day, Daisy taught me the importance of self-care, self-respect and treating myself as very special. I am going to throw out my motley panama collection and make a conscious choice concerning my nightwear. I would not only like them to feel good but also to feel glamorous on me even when no one is watching!

Process

*Looking for endings
I often get started
toward something
going somewhere
getting nowhere.
This older heart
beats wiser now.
I remember springtime
passion ardor
beginnings
Death will not find me
Seated!*

5

> "Art rests upon a kind of religious sense,
> a deep, immutable earnestness."
>
> *Johann Wolfgang von Goethe*

Ernie came into Daisy's Treasure Trove again today while I was working alone. He inquired about Daisy and I told him that she would not be back in the store until Friday. "Do you still have the wooden parrots that I saw the last time I was here?" He gestured towards the doorway leading into the clothing room.

"Yes, Ernie, they're hanging on that wheel to the right of the doorway. They're there so people will not bump their heads on them," I responded.

"Oh good! I want the green one because my cockatoo needs a friend. I'll be back later on to pay for it," he smiled and added, "Did you get any bigger belts in?" I went to look once more and there were none. "I'll be back later in the week to check," he remarked and headed out the door. I believe that he enjoyed his visit with Daisy and me on the previous Saturday and that he decided to come back for more frivolity. This revelation made me smile in the quiet moments after his exit.

Rick came in soon after Ernie's exit to place the rocking chair outside of the door and to check the thermostat. It had not been working well and Daisy had pointed that out to him. He seated himself into one of the chairs and I could sense that he wanted to chat. I had a pile of clothing to put away on hangers and I told him that I had to finish my chores in a short time period, but that he could keep talking while I worked.

"I feel very anxious today, Sandra, even though I have walked along the ocean a few times. I don't seem to be able to settle," he opened the conversation. I chose to stay silent and focused on putting the clothes onto hangers. He spoke of many things, and it was difficult to concentrate because I needed to complete the task that I had set my mind to. I was also being careful not to function as a therapist.

I did feel that his anxiety was fear based. He was beginning to ask himself some important existential questions that come up again and again for many of us as we make our way through life's passages.

"I don't know what I should be doing now that my wife has passed and our dreams were dashed," he went on.

I also knew that like me, he was experiencing a complicated grieving. He was not only into loss but liberation at the same time. I stayed silent as I witnessed him making the twists and turns in his mind and speaking in streams of consciousness. I made the conscious choice of high witnessing him because I felt that he was looking for answers from me that I did not have. I was asking life questions myself. I was into a radical separation from old ways of being in the world that no longer served me.

Early, in my career as a psychotherapist, I believed that I was supposed to have the answers for what I now consider deeply spiritual questions. I have been a victim of 'stump the therapist' too many times by many who wanted to solidify their defenses and often felt burned out. I was not a savior, but the role had been imposed upon me, as well as assumed by me since my childhood. I was learning to become full of care for myself and I no longer felt that I was selfish but rather becoming self-full. I needed to give up that superiority, as well, that comes with the savior mentality and role, as well as the self-sacrifice that had been handed down for generations by the women in my relational past.

Endings bring new beginnings. I learned over time and through personal introspection and processing that it takes an incredible amount of courage to face the darkness and move towards the light of consciousness. That was not something I wanted to engage in with Rick. I made a conscious choice not to.

"I respect your non assuming ways and professional behavior," he commented and left the store with his questions. He would have to live into the answers and I would have to work on letting him without running too much interference.

Johnny arrived for his daily apple and to check on me. He was very serious about wanting me to know about the store and Daisy's protocol. He takes Daisy very seriously and likes to assist her in any way that he can.

Two young women who had been in the store on Saturday and bought a pair of blue and white sling-back shoes came in to browse as Rick appeared at the door, once again offering to bring me a cup of coffee. I graciously accepted. He informed me that he was going to take another walk along the ocean. The young women bought a few pieces of retro-jewelry and left the store smiling. I was certain that I would see them again.

Rick brought me the coffee and ended up seeing a scarf on the shelf that matched his jacket. He bought it. "The wind has a chill in it and it will soon be time for us to bundle up," he remarked before he headed for the ocean.

It was closing time and Ernie returned with his cash for the green parrot and made a promise that he would return soon.

I closed the store and felt such gratitude for the changes that were taking place in my life. I had listened to my heart when I came to volunteer for Daisy. I was realizing that I was being put into direct alignment with those teachings and teachers who sought to come into my awareness. Unknowingly perhaps, I extended an invitation to Daisy to help me on my spiritual journey back to my authentic self. I recognized that everyone who comes into our lives can take us deeper into knowing ourselves if we are willing. They can represent light or dark forces depending on the lessons.

I wanted my personal relationship with my new male friend Garth, to be one of high consciousness but an intersection of primary vulnerabilities was taking place between us. I had no clear sense of what was beginning to happen; only that he had begun to remind me of my father and his military ways. His communication style was that of interrogator and instructor and I experienced his behavior as possessive and controlling towards me. I did not like the pain I was experiencing. This was too much of a re-play of my painful past in my father's house where the women were made obedient to the dictates of the dominant culture.

Was it that I needed to see him as controlling so that I did not have to face past pain and could project it onto him, or was ten percent of what I was feeling relevant to the present and ninety percent emotional flashbacks to the past? These were pressing questions for me, and I was feeling frightened.

Whenever I felt frightened as a girl, I would run over to my grandmother's house. She created a room for me to stay in and I had a card table set up so that I could write. It was in that room that I dreamed of becoming a writer or a journalist. I isolated myself with my fears and would end up beside my grandparents' bed on the floor in the morning. I did not know how to express my fears or ask for soothing. My grandfather would find me first and say in his British accent, "Aye love, what are you doing down there again?" He would tell me to get into the bed beside my grandmother. It felt wonderful to snuggle into her warm body.

I did what I was told to do for fifty years and when I chose to come back to what I felt was my calling, I unconsciously sabotaged my success in order to stay connected to my family. I did not respect my talents or my work and spent too much time making apologies. This behavior led me to be totally disconnected from my true self. My parents obviously believed in a 'punishing God' ideology, and I was reprimanded over and over again for any kind of personal expression. This kept me close to them at a terrible expense to myself. I repeated the pattern of the dutiful daughter many times until it nearly broke me physically, emotionally, mentally and spiritually. I recognized that I stayed close to them because of my need for their approval and enforced dependency. I knew that I could not do that anymore. I had to become a 'myth buster'.

Heroics

*She learned early to cloak the pain
to become tied to tomorrows
and promises of more joy in heaven.
Haunted by ' what ifs and if onlys'
the faded robe of middle age
signaled the mourning that would
expose a mythology hung in varnished
pictures of tight smiles and pretense
on walls that held no truth.*

6

"For while the tale of how we suffer, how we are delighted and how we triumph is never new, it always must be heard. There isn't any other tale to tell. It is the only light that we have in the darkness."

James Baldwin

It was the feast of 'All Hallows' also known as Halloween. I decided to dress like a black priestess. She has been linked to the ancient black Madonna archetype in that she represents wisdom and that part of us that gets us across the street in traffic. She is considered a good witch. I wore a long, black velvet dress and a hat that was decorated with a feather and a black rose. I also wanted to represent the archetype of the Crone, in the sense that I was moving into a stronger personal identification with that energy in my sixties.

Daisy came to work looking radiant in an orange skirt, black vest, and black pants. She wore pumpkin earrings and her lipstick matched her shirt. I marveled at her beauty and passion just as I had at my mother in my early years. Rick entered soon after we arrived and shared that he had slept until eleven o'clock. I commented, "You must have needed it."

"Well," he started a confession. "I was up until the wee hours of the morning at a local pub and I got carried away. You know, when everyone is drinking, one does not realize how many one has imbibed!"

"Not a good thing to do, Rick!" Daisy exclaimed. Rick looked a little sheepish, recognizing perhaps that he was not going to get any pity at this party.

"I walked a police woman home who was very chatty. I really can show good manners, Daisy."

I chuckled and Daisy whispered into my ear, "Rick has to raise the bar. He has a lot to learn yet." She was grinning from ear to ear.

A middle-aged couple came into the store at this point. The gentleman was looking for a Corning Ware bowl. I got up from my chair to assist him in the china and appliance section. We found a lid first and then located a bowl that would hold it. He was elated because he told us that he wanted to cook a chicken recipe for friends that afternoon. His wife was searching through things in the clothing section and came out to the counter with a couple of items and a big smile on her face.

I was behind the counter with Daisy at this point and Daisy was speaking to the woman's husband. He was in the process of helping Daisy to get some donations so that she could keep the store going. The woman watched Daisy very carefully and I witnessed tears welling up in her eyes. She looked at me, and I smiled as we shared a very spiritual moment together. I believe that we were both appreciating who Daisy was. She winked at me through her tears, then she and her husband left and I believe she was filled with Daisy's light. A woman of ninety-one years stood in front of us. She was lucid, vibrant and obviously did not miss a trick!

A pun intended on this Halloween day!

Daisy asked me to sit with her a while and offered to tell me more of her story.

"Tell me about your first love, Daisy." I had so much to ask yet.

"I was married when I was seventeen. That was not young in those days because we were under the impression as girls that you would be called a spinster if you had not found a man to marry before your twenties. I married my first boyfriend just before the war broke out. I had two children, Deanna and Barry with him. My husband went overseas and we were separated by the war so long that he met another woman and we were divorced."

"That must have been extremely difficult for you," I remarked.

"I don't really remember. We got a small pension when our men were overseas and it must have been adequate because I was able to dress my little ones well and take care of myself. My husband was the second of three boys and a girl, and I don't believe as I look back now, that he was ready for married life. Life changed so quickly in those years. I seemed to get through okay. I have always been a fighter and I fought my way through it."

I had recognized that spunk in Daisy the first time that I met her. I hope that it does take one to know one because I have felt admiration for her so many times since. I seemed to have to fight my way through some very difficult circumstances as well.

I asked her to tell me about her initiatives in White Rock.

"Another woman who is still alive called me to inquire about any interest I might have in taking over a house where a woman had recently passed away. She wanted me to partner with her. We were aware of a need that handicapped people had who had recently been put into institutions like Riverview and Woodland. They seemed to have nowhere to go. The government wouldn't give us the funding but it was suggested that they might give us a grant. We applied and got one for two years and then we moved to the present Charlie Don't Surf restaurant and stayed at that location for ten years. White Rock started to grow and the landlords started inflating rents. A Chinese woman came into the store every month with an envelope for my rent. One day she came to inform me that it was going up to four thousand a month." Daisy was adamant that I quote the woman exactly: "You good tenant pay rent, stay."

Daisy added, "I thought it over and I decided that it was time to move elsewhere. If I was such a good tenant then she could have kept the rent the same. The electricity bill was very high as well. I found this place right here and I have been down here for seventeen years now. At first we leased only half of this store," she pointed to the section where we were sitting that held some jewelry, some clothes, toys, knick-knacks and the appliances up the stairs. I asked her to tell me more. "The man that had the other half of the store went bankrupt and the landlords wanted me to take it over too, but the rent was way too high. I held out for five months and the owners rented it to me at my price." She grinned from ear to ear.

I told her that I needed to know more about her project in its beginning and so she began. "We were registered in Victoria as The Modern Service Club for the Handicapped. We had all kinds of people coming to us from Riverview and Woodland for arts and crafts. It became more of a teaching place for the handicapped in terms of learning to socialize, exploring their creativity and refining their life skills. We wanted to assist them out there in the world. We had many retired teachers come in to volunteer and we sometimes serviced twenty to thirty people at a time. Some of the challenged were diagnosed with developmental problems, as well as mental illness. Some were bipolar, schizophrenic, and car accident victims who had suffered brain injuries. We did not turn anyone away who needed help. The courts sent younger boys too who had been caught with marijuana, or had stolen things from stores or taken cars."

"Has that changed over time, Daisy?" I was getting bits and pieces about her journey and I knew that the story would come together in time.

"Most of the people who work with me now are challenged mentally and have been in recovery a long time. I struggled so much with the rules set down by the government that I decided that it would be better for everyone concerned to create a board of directors. We started with eight partners and have six on the board now. The government wanted to assign a person to run the show. I saw it as someone sitting back and watching while we ran into bankruptcy. The board still has a meeting once a year now and I give a financial report. I usually end up having to call the meeting. All of the money that comes in goes to the rent, electricity and the telephone. Sometimes we don't acquire enough money for the rent. Right now we have to take in $40.00 a day to survive and often I am short. Sometimes we, the members of the board, have had to use our own money for the rent payment. We have never had money from the government as most people think. Visitors don't come to the store as much as they used to because of the parking problem in White Rock. I only care about working with the people sent to me and that is my thing. At this very moment, Sandra, I am two hundred dollars short for the rent this month."

"Thank you, Daisy, for this part of your story; I have a much better sense of your mission." I was moved by her story so far and felt more dedicated than ever to finish the book.

Rick came into the store with his green coffee cup just as I finished interviewing Daisy. He said that he had been down at the ocean for one of his daily walks. He promised his wife before she passed that he would spread her ashes on the beach and walk there everyday in fond remembrance. He was eager to tell Daisy and me something as he shifted from one foot to the other smiling. "I learned from someone on the beach that one is able to Google White Rock and I'm in the scan at the corner of Marine Drive and Vidal Street with my green cup. The person who informed me asked me if I was the guy with the green cup." He continued telling us about his experience of someone coming along and offering to put money into his green cup.

"What was that all about, Rick?" I questioned.

"Well, a sea lion had been dead for three days on the beach last summer. The smell was becoming a health hazard and the restaurant owners were up in arms about it. I was at the White Rock Museum when there was filming going on and people were coming in while there was mention of the sea lion problem. They wanted to put money in the coffee cup to help have the smell situation alleviated." He started to laugh then and said, "I told the people that I could not accept the money or the responsibility." He was grinning at me, "I should have had some pencils with me."

"Why is that?" I asked naively.

"Do you know what a busker is?"

Daisy interjected now, "The people coming into the museum were under the impression that Rick was a bum!" I chuckled at her statement, and she looked at me with a sheepish grin.

Rick attempted to explain more to me. "They are legitimized pan handlers."

Daisy began to sing, "Hallelujah I'm a Bum" and she sang all of the lyrics of that song for Rick. I never know what I am going to learn through play or humor when I am graced by the presence of Daisy and Rick. It is usually memorable. I had a sense that Rick was becoming more self-conscious each day that he visited Daisy in my presence. I wanted to believe that all of his anecdotes seemed to carry meta messages that he was attempting to sort out his life since losing his wife of thirty years. I wanted to believe that he was attempting to find some kind of community and support system. Spiritual issues were coming up for him to sort through and it seemed that he was processing them through his everyday experiences and relating them to Daisy for comment. Daisy always welcomed him through her jokes, stories, songs, gifts and laughter.

"There is a regular crowd at the beach now when I walk," he commented. "There is acknowledgement even if it is only a reminder to 'sockey up on a cold day'." Rick left us with the intention of getting dressed early for the Halloween festivities so that we could see him in costume. A young man entered at that point looking for a costume. He headed for the clothing section while I interviewed Daisy.

"Daisy, would you tell me more about what you did when you were helping the special needs people." I wanted clarity. She was happy to continue.

"We took busloads of them to ball games many times to give

them an outing. That was fun. I often had to report boarding homes for not feeding them properly."

The young man, Daniel, came out of the clothing room into the space where Daisy and I were sitting. I knew that he had been listening and watching us. "I am sorry to interrupt, but do you have any masks?"

I went to the front window to get one. There was only one and it was of a devil's face. He tried it on, and even though the eyeholes did not match his eye spaces he thought that it might suit the occasion. He told us that his girlfriend wanted him to dress up for the festivities. Daisy said that there was a devil's suit hung with the costumes in the other room so I obliged him once again by retrieving a red top and leggings. It was obvious that the outfit was made for a child but he said that he would give the tights a try. When he headed for the dressing room, Daisy and I just smiled at one another.

It was a day for men in tights! Our customer came back to us, "I believe that the tights might just do the trick, but I will need a shirt to match."

I went on another search and found a red plaid long sleeved shirt in the men's section, and he left again for the dressing room. It didn't take long for him to come out to model for us. The shirt suited the tights and there wasn't much time left to be choosy.

"I would like to browse just a bit more, if you don't mind," he implored looking worried. Within minutes he eyed a dress on the clothing rack for larger women. It was black with gold ribbing down the front, around the neck, and the bottom of the dress. I had brought it in that very day because someone had given it to me as a gift and it was too big for me.

"I think that you are on to something," I commented. He headed for the dressing room once again then he exited with the dress on. It just covered his kneecaps. I burst out laughing because I scanned his profile and noticed that he was still wearing his short socks and running shoes. He was a picture to be beheld in that dress!

I was flooded for a few moments with memories of helping my children to dress for Halloween. I am not sure that my youngest son has ever forgiven me for dressing him up with a wig, jewelry and a dress. He was only four years old at the time, and I have put that picture up with the three of them every Halloween since. This young man showed no signs of embarrassment and seemed to be having a great time modeling for two older women.

He was right into having fun, "Do you have anything else that would help me to pull this sorcerer thing off?" I remembered a gold neckpiece with a silver tie and I located it in the costume box. Daisy pointed to a wig on the counter and it resembled a toupee when he put it on his head. (I am laughing out loud now as I write this!)

He modeled for us. "I like it!" I also found a plastic sword in the costume box and he transformed into a wizard. He went to change into his street clothes and Daisy and I were bent over laughing.

He came out to us again and said, "I decided that I will take both the devil and the sorcerer outfits and see which one my girl friend likes the best." He paid six dollars for the goods and he had himself a wonderful hour of entertainment with two elder women who admired his good nature and his willingness to enter into an unfolding drama. I hoped that he would come back and tell us how he fared.

Rick was coming in the door just as Daniel was leaving and thanking us for an experience that he would never forget. Now, we had Rick modeling for us and I had to take some pictures. He had chosen to wear a pair of black silk shorts instead of the tights. I must say that I felt deep in my bones that he also had a wonderful Halloween at Daisy's.

Halleluiah, Rick!

7

"The best thing I can do as an artist is to disturb."
Liza Minnelli

It was not my day to work at Daisy's, but I was feeling that I needed more time to spend with her in order to get more of her story.

Soon after I arrived at the store, a young woman came in to speak with Daisy. She introduced herself as Kirsten, a worker from one of the Lodges. She wanted Daisy to mentor Betty whom she introduced to both of us. Daisy offered Betty the opportunity to work with me on Wednesdays when I usually worked alone.

"Sandra can show you the ropes," Daisy looked at me.

"I'll be glad to do that, Daisy, if you trust me that much."

Betty's face lit up then, "I'd like to work here," she responded.

The new recruit headed for the clothing room as Kirsten continued her conversation with Daisy. Betty returned to the counter where we stood within minutes. She had located a green flannel pullover and red running shoes.

"How much for these, Daisy?" she inquired.

"The shirt cost one dollar and put the shoes in your bag where I don't see them," Daisy met her eyes with benevolence.

"The shoes don't have any laces," Betty quipped.

Kirsten said, "That's the style now."

Daisy added, "That will be a good mission for you now to find the perfect laces." I made myself busy hanging up clothes that had been left outside of the store the night before. Betty found me and her eyes were full of longing.

"I think I'd like a pair of jeans." I took her to the pant section where she immediately found a pair of denim pull-on jeans. She looked so pleased and took them out to the main section to show Kirsten. I guess that she felt that she needed some kind of permission.

"I don't think that they'll fit you," Kirsten commented.

"I think they will," Betty retorted. I took them from her and put them up in front of her hips and waist.

"You might like to try them." I pointed the way to the dressing room.

Daisy instructed Kirsten now, "Let her find something that she really likes and let her have her joy; she will figure it out."

I heard a faint pleading from the dressing room area, "Will someone please help me?" I went to look and found Betty in her underpants with one leg partially into one pant-leg and the pants were backwards. I went to her aid and helped her to get the jeans on. She was not embarrassed in the least and slipped right out of the dressing room to model them for Kirsten.

"I was right you see! They fit perfectly!"

Daisy was beaming now. "You see how happy that has made her, Kirsten?"

I witnessed a woman having real pleasure and packed the three treasures for her into a bag. Betty went straight to the door ready to leave.

"Wait a minute! I'm not finished yet," Kirsten, reprimanded her.

"She's so happy to covet her new things," I smiled.

"Do you need a smoke?" Kirsten went on.

"No, I was in a hurry to put my things on," Betty replied sheepishly.

Betty re-entered the store and stood right in front of Daisy. "Are you a hundred yet?" She questioned.

"No, not yet," Daisy answered. "But I do intend to live that long."

"Well, you are so beautiful, and so are you, Sandra," she gifted us both. I was honored and amazed at this wonderful commentary on the part of a woman well into her sixties who was considered developmentally delayed and depressed most of her life.

Getting ready to exit with Kirsten, Betty added, "I look forward to working for you on Wednesdays, Sandra."

Rick entered for the first time that day and I knew that there would be other visits. He wanted to inform Daisy that he intended to put a handicap security bar in the bathroom to make things easier for her. He always showed good intention.

Daisy pointed out, "It's silly to do anything too complicated now if the landlords are soon going to be tearing the building down. I can handle it the way it is for now."

"Yes, Daisy, I know, but you need assistance now and that's what concerns me the most. I don't want you to fall getting off or onto the toilet, especially when you're alone in the store," he retorted.

Daisy made no further comments. It was nearing closing time and it had been a rather full day. Although we did not have a lot of interview time, a story was in the process of unfolding moment to moment. I was getting to know Daisy through my direct experience of her and through high witnessing her ministrations to those who came into her presence.

8

> "I put my hand in yours and together we can
> do what each of us can't do alone."
>
> *Helen Keller*

The first Tuesday in November was a beautiful day. I finished my household rituals and did two hours of writing. I had also sorted through my closets for some things for Daisy's store. I am trying to travel lighter and easier now. But re-cycling is also fun for me. I was looking more forward to seeing Daisy as the days passed. Community seemed to happen there, and I was feeling a deep sense of belonging in her presence and with those who knew and respected her.

I felt like an outcast most of my life, and have come to recognize that it had to do with a uniqueness of character that I possessed that my parents had difficulty relating to. Just like the 'Ugly Duckling' motif, perhaps I was a swan trying to find my identity and worth in a pack of ducks. I am not saying that there is anything wrong with ducks either! I had internalized the message, however, that 'difference' was a bad thing and I spent a great deal of my past feeling a deep sense of unworthiness and shame. I certainly felt unlovable and tried every contortion of self to keep connection and to feel a sense of belonging. I found myself moving out of an old matrix and coming of age in White Rock through the kinship I had with Daisy. Could it be that I had found a swan mother? It seemed to take such little effort to be with her and I could speak so honestly and freely! I felt a deep sense of belonging with her.

It was '$1.49 Tuesday' and Jane who was under Daisy's mentorship, was busy vacuuming. The vacuum is an archaic old clunker and one could hardly hear oneself speak when it was motoring! It seemed to me that Jane was acting very mechanically and she did not acknowledge me at all. She looked as though she was 'numbed out'.

Two women were at the counter when I arrived. They introduced themselves above the din of the vacuum cleaner. Lorre, from Maple Ridge, and Miranda, from Pitt Meadows, had found a number of treasures that Daisy had already put into a bag for them before I arrived. Lorre spontaneously gave Miranda a big hug and thanked her profusely for bringing her to Daisy's Treasure Trove especially on '$1.49 day'. She pulled a pair of shoes out of her bag just to show me. Daisy pointed out that those shoes were new and worth $189.00. Lorre bought them for $1.49. After that, these ladies were so proud to show me all of their wares and share their excitement with me. It seemed that we were a pack of women howling now with glee! Daisy stood as high witness to this and laughed heartily, too.

A British woman with her teenage daughter entered next. They headed for the clothing section and returned to the counter with nine pieces of clothing. Daisy had seated herself on her favorite chair and was eating her usual mid-day half of a sandwich so I was in charge of the sales. They wanted to see some jewelry and this led to quite an experience of feminine ritual. The mother was into retro-earrings and bought five pair after receiving her daughter's approval. Her daughter chose a broach that simulated an old watch and chain. They became very animated in the exchange of opinion and mirroring. For $20.39 they had a wonderful new wardrobe and accessories. How good can it get? I felt sadness then knowing that I never had this kind of quality time with my mother or my daughter.

Daisy now had some time to talk. "Sandra, I have learned

more in this store in the last two years than I have most of my years in this work." I wanted more clarity about her early days of her work with the disenfranchised.

"How long did you get the government grant?" I began the questions.

"For just the two years, and then a group of us created the Board. I was in my fifties when I opened. I have yet to tell you my experiences before that," she added.

"I am looking forward to that, Daisy," I responded.

"You know, Sandra, that I have many pictures on the wall of Marilyn Monroe and I feel a need to tell you now about that experience." Daisy led the way now. "She was on the set of 'River of No Return' with Rory Calhoun. I will have to save that for another day, though."

Rick was making his way through the doorway once again. He was fervent in his attempt to get the bathroom in order for Daisy. I had to chuckle as he explained, "The bar that Bob gave me did not measure with the wall studs."

He thought that the landlord might have a pole for her to grip instead of the bar he had. "Are you ready to do some pole dancing, Daisy?" he goaded her. Daisy just smiled back. It was near closing time and Rick left saying that he would be in the next day. Seeing behind his illusions, Daisy smiled sardonically and said, "I'm sure you will be."

Robert, the landlord, came in right then with the pole and a bag of donations for the store. He told Daisy that he had spoken to Rick about the pole and Daisy silently shook her head. Two men were offering her assistance and compassion and wanted her to be comfortable on her throne! These were the same gifts that she had granted to so many over the years. It was her turn to be on the receiving end. Like so many women, receiving was and still is more difficult than giving. What about these daughters of Eve with their intrinsic sense of unworthiness?

Perhaps a myth-busting is due. What if we could view Eve as an awakening woman who was tired and angry from life in Paradise?

Was she a kept woman and supposed to be satisfied with eating, defecating, sleeping and fornicating? Was it an inner demand for consciousness that she was feeling that led her to decide to eat from the tree of knowledge and springboard her evolution? The snake, the symbol of consciousness, was in the garden the whole time! Did she long to have her lover join with her in those discoveries? Was her only sin that of revealing the dark side of a punishing God ideology? What if she might have been depressed because she was feeling oppressed? There was no Prozac in the Garden!

Do many women on the Earth Walk exist with a deep sense of shame and inferiority because Eve was seen as dangerous to the status quo? Why was she made the outcast? Could it be that women too, are the 'Word' made flesh and dwell amongst us?

These are good questions and may we become curious and brave enough to live into the answers!

Daisy spoke adamantly now. "I don't need a pole to help me on and off the toilet. I don't understand your focus on that need." She moved deliberately towards the counter pushing past Robert. "I need to get this store ready for closing now!"

I couldn't help but notice her emphasis on the need for closure.

9

"Every meeting of persons is a gift wrapped by the Creator because they will eventually move you deeper into the knowledge of yourself if you are willing to grow."

Dawna Markova

It was another beautiful fall day in White Rock, and it was my day on duty at Daisy's. I was intent on getting to the store early to initiate Betty into Daisy's protocol. Daisy had asked me to put the Halloween decorations away and I thought that this was a good first task for my initiate. She arrived earlier than expected because she was so excited to get started. Betty helped me with the Halloween clearing, and then I asked her to help me to sort some of the items in the store that needed to be displayed differently. She worked diligently with me and seemed to really enjoy it.

A man came into the store with five other people. I sensed right away that he was a social worker dealing with the mentally challenged. He introduced himself as Brian and shared with me that he had known Daisy for many years. I told him that I was writing Daisy's story. He was adamant that I just listen and not write anything until he was finished telling me his story about Daisy.

"One day I was at the beach for a long time with several clients from Britannia and I decided to take them down into Daisy's store. She was so pleased that we had come to her store and she insisted that she buy them all ice cream from the store next door. Now who would be so kind? Only Daisy Walls!"

In the meantime, those in his charge were circling around the store searching for treasures. One of the men introduced himself as Roy and told me that he would like a radio. I found a small transistor radio on the shelf. He was ecstatic! He also wanted a wind-up watch. I had to disappoint him because there were none to be had. He recognized Betty just then and leaned to hug her. Brian walked by at that time and said, "Roy, don't hug the ladies."

Roy answered back now, "Brian, I have known this lady for many, many years, and I am so happy to see her again!" He looked at Betty and implored, "Would you like to have dinner with me sometime, Betty?"

She responded with, "Sure, Roy, that would be nice."

I witnessed an act of true appreciation and caring much like Daisy's story about her connection and the hug with the native woman from Whitehorse. It was a heart connection!

Another woman, introduced by Brian as Mary, had been looking at the goods from Guatemala and had already put on two of the ankle bracelets. She came over to pay me $5.00. She moved into the clothing section where one of her male friends, Garant, was sorting through the jeans. It did not take her long to find a long bohemian style dress that she modeled for her friend and purchased for $2.00. Garant found a pair of jeans for $4.00. They were two happy customers!

Roy was ready to pay up and got his radio for $2.00.

Brian was at the counter next with a record he had found and wondered if I could help him choose a gift for his sister. I showed him some broaches that would appeal to me because he had said that she was my age. My first choice was a gold plated cougar and he thought he could trust my taste. This discovery led Brian to check that he might find something for his brother but nothing seemed to suit the occasion. Brian's treasures came to a grand total of $8.00 and he gave me ten for Daisy's cause. He gathered up his charges saying, "Don't forget to tell Daisy that I was in to see her and that I promise to be back soon."

Rick came through the door at the same time as their exit offering to help me to take out the garbage and to put things into Daisy's 'free box' that sat outside the front door. We had quite a few laughs together as we sorted and pitched commenting on the various items that needed to be thrown out. So many times I had to ask Rick what some of the items were used for. He just rolled his eyes and held the bag for the 'free box' open for me to dump the junk.

A lady came into the store to browse in the meantime and left with three sweaters that I had brought in that morning for recycling. She had a hundred dollar bill that I could not change and so, I sent her to Annie's Beach Mart across the street and told her to tell Annie that I sent her. She came back beaming since Annie was more than happy to oblige her and to help Daisy. She bought the sweaters and made a new friend at the same time!

Betty had put in her required two hours and got ready to leave. As she was walking out the door she looked at me and said, "Sandra, I really enjoyed my day here and I feel really good about myself."

Mission accomplished, Daisy!

I felt full and happy when closing time came. I had another day of hearing and helping those who knew and loved Daisy for a very long time.

10

> "Although the world is full of suffering,
> it is also full of overcoming it."
>
> *Helen Keller*

On Saturdays I work with Daisy and my assignment this day was to create a Veterans' Day window display. Daisy instructed me to find a navy jacket in the men's wear area and to pin a poppy on the lapel. I did as requested. Daisy thought that we should find the lapel pins that represent Canada. We started a treasure hunt through several boxes and then I remembered having seen something with several pins on it. It took a few minutes and Daisy was able to locate a tie that held several pins representing the Canadian Provinces. I placed the tie with the pins in the window. We thought that more poppies might be good.

Of course, Rick happened to 'pop' in at just the right time and said that he could pick up some at the Semiahmoo Mall. He left and Daisy commented, "It would be wonderful if we had some pictures of men and women in uniform."

My dad had been in the Royal Canadian Regiment and had served in eight campaigns in Europe as a lieutenant. I had some pictures at home and I told Daisy that I would bring some in the next day. She said, "I would like to put a picture in the window of my sister in uniform."

I had written a book titled, "Tracking the Predator" in which

I gave tribute to my dad. I proudly displayed the book opened to the dedication to him. Rick returned with the poppies and the window coming together just as we were, for whatever reasons!

A couple came in with their two young adolescent daughters from Vernon. They were visiting and had just left the pier where they had set some crab traps. Daisy told them about using chicken parts to lure them and we all had a laugh. The girls played soccer and Daisy asked them if they would be interested in soccer cards because we got a bagful the day before. They said that they were not into collecting cards of any kind. I saw that they really enjoyed Daisy's humor, and they said they would be back when they were this way again.

Daisy asked me to sit beside her then because she brought some special cream with her to rub my hands. So, here I was now receiving care and encouragement when I was so used to taking care. It felt wonderful to be ministered to. A ninety-one year old woman was offering to nurture me. It brought tears to my eyes as I tapped into some grief around missing mother care in my life and as a result of that, missing my own pain and attending to others.

I suffer from psoriatic arthritis and Daisy is adamant that I am going to get free of it. In fact, after her ministrations, I forgot about the pain in my hands. Energy gets blocked when a child attempts to reach out and no one is available physically or emotionally. I have learned, as well that the psycho-emotional component of arthritis is self-blame.

Rick made another entrance to discuss putting a pole in the bathroom to assist Daisy and she got very firm with him saying, "I told you a pole is not going to work." Rick retorted, "I am going to do something about that grip near the toilet whether you like it or not. I don't want you to fall."

He left again and a beautiful woman in her eighties came in to buy the rocking chair that Rick had been moving for three weeks. I knew he would be relieved. Daisy sold it to her for $15.00. The original price was $75.00.

Daisy's daughter, Patty, usually picks her up after work but this night my friend and I gave her a ride home. Daisy pointed the way to her house and asked me in for a moment to see the sitting room and her two cats, Emma and Kizzy. She was so proud to show me what a modular home was like. I was very impressed and privileged to be invited into her personal space that she shared with her daughter Patty.

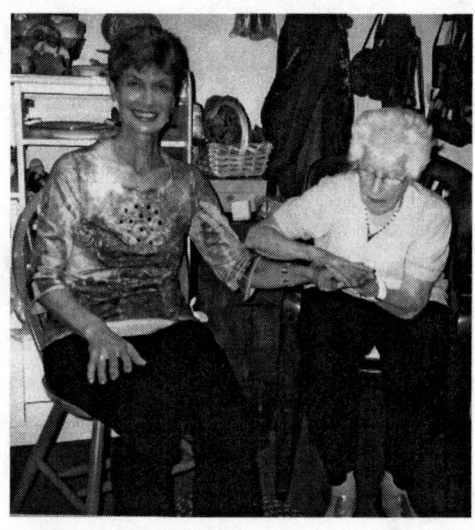

11

"We can do no great things – only small things with great love."
Mother Teresa.

It is another Sunday at Daisy's, and because I wanted to get more of her story, I went in to volunteer for the afternoon. When I arrived Daisy introduced me to her two helpers for the day. She said, "This is Stacey, Sandra, who has known me for six years and this is Winnie, who has been with me for thirty years." They both stood to shake my hand in greeting.

Winnie offered, "I lived with Daisy for several years."

"Yes," Daisy added, "her step-father was mean especially after her mother died and I helped her to get out. She had to climb out of her bedroom window to escape."

"If it wasn't for Daisy, I would have been out on the street," Winnie smiled affectionately at Daisy.

"Yes, she fooled him and got out!" Daisy affirmed Winnie.

Soon after the introductions, two young women arrived and went straight to Daisy who was now seated in her big chair. Their names, I learned, were Kerri and Cindy-Lou. They had lived above Daisy's store when it was on Marine Drive.

Cindy-Lou looked at Daisy and said, "My, Daisy, you are looking well. When I first came in I told myself that I knew that woman, and then I saw your eyes and knew it was you. I am so sorry that I have not been in to see you for a while. I have a new business at home and it has kept me so busy."

Daisy responded, "You will have to bring me a sample of what you have now and maybe I can get some orders here."

Cindy-Lou explained that she was selling flip-flops that were made out of all natural products and that they were excellent for beach wear. Kerri began talking to Daisy as Cindy-Lou went to the clothing section to browse. Kerri complimented Daisy in terms of how bright she looked and turned to me.

"She has helped so many who were struggling over the years. She has always had a happy disposition."

Cindy-Lou came back into the room where Daisy was seated and turned to address me.

"She used to have a 'Five Dollar Armload Sale' and all my friends would come to the store with me and laugh and giggle the whole time we were hunting for treasures. It was always a good deal, but the best part was the fun we had with Daisy." She eyed a scarf close by and wrapped it around her head. Daisy said that Cindy Lou looked like Hiawatha and she wanted me to take a picture but my camera was out of film. "That's okay, Daisy, I will come by later in the week wearing the scarf but better groomed!"

Kerri returned with a black and silver scarf and asked Cindy-Lou to lend her some money but it cost only $2.00 and she had enough cash to pay for it.

Kerri stepped towards me and shared, "This lady has always been a strong member of society and so helpful and inspirational."

I knew at some deeper level that these two young women were here to show their love and respect to a woman who has been a role model of feminine development for them. It warmed my heart knowing that there is such a longing in young women for just that; in fact, we all need many mothers. It is all too much for one's personal mother to contain the archetype of the Great Mother.

The young women left with a promise to return soon and hugged both Daisy and me.

Winnie witnessed what was happening and began to share a

story with me, "I always bring a chicken and bologna sandwich and milk for Daisy when I come. She really likes the sandwich."

"So you and Daisy have a little ritual when you come in," I affirmed her.

"Yes, anything for my sweet Daisy." She could not stop praising the woman who helped her to maintain her vital life. In fact, just that day, Daisy made her come in to help in the store even though she had a broken arm. Daisy told me on the sly, "I feel that by getting Winnie out, she will not be at home feeling sorry for herself and getting depressed."

"You see, Winnie, you have had a good time today and a few laughs."

"Yes, Daisy," she said. "You are right, my sweet, Daisy; this has been good for me, you are my angel." Daisy could not quite hear the angel part and asked her to repeat it and when she did, Daisy flapped her arms like a bird.

Ernie came in at that point looking for some socks and Winnie went with him to the sock drawer in the clothing room. They came back and Ernie waved his white and brown socks in front of Daisy. He seemed very pleased with his treasures and Winnie was proud to have found them for him. He sat for a few minutes to visit. "I am cooking for myself again and I have a chicken in the oven right now that I need to attend to."

"I hope it doesn't dry out like your roast," Daisy said. I remembered that he talked about cooking a roast the last time that he was in.

"What happened, Ernie?" I was curious.

Daisy interceded, "He didn't put any liquid in the roaster and the roast and the potatoes were bone dry."

Ernie went on, "Daisy, you wouldn't happen to have a pressure cooker for sale?"

"Good luck with that," she replied. "No one uses them any more."

"What do you want one for, Ernie?" I asked.

"I want to make pork hocks and sauerkraut and I like the meat to fall off the bones. The only way I learned to do this was using a pressure cooker."

"What about just slow cooking them," I offered.

"Yes," Daisy said, "and put some water in with them!"

Daisy asked Winnie to look for the "Cookbook for Dummies" and said that Ernie would probably like that. My heart took a flip! Daisy made it clear to him then that she was not implying that he was a dummy, "I just want to make it simpler for you." Winnie found the book and Daisy said, "It is a Christmas present to you, Ernie."

Ernie declined saying, "I think I will leave the cooking to my sister-in-law as much as possible. I have to go now and rake the leaves."

"You are getting too old for that. Just leave them until they have all dropped off and do it one time only," Daisy was ministering to him again. "You need to take better care of yourself."

He got up out of his chair, "I best get home, but I want you to keep an eye out for those snap button shirts and suspenders."

It was closing time again and Patty came to drive Winnie and Daisy home. I locked up the store and smiled as I crossed the street remembering the humor, the compassion and the love shared in the day.

I felt very grateful in the quiet moments going home.

12

> "There are some violent acts that pierce the atmosphere of one's life leaving a hole through which the damp wind seems to blow forever. It comes up again and again."
>
> *Xinran*

Johnny was rolling pennies when I entered Daisy's. I remembered that Daisy had told me that he loved that process and that she had him do it as often as she could. He was looking very disheveled but content.

"How are you today, Johnny?" I usually made the overture.

"Fine, Sandra. How are you?" he connected.

I tried to engage him right away and asked him about his past. He shared, "My father was a drummer and my mother was a singer. My father left when I was three years old and I could not stay with my mother. I was in foster care most of my life."

"Where do you live now, Johnny?"

"I live at the Lodge."

"Did you go to school?" I wanted to know more about this young man that Daisy had taken under her wings.

"I went to school in North Surrey, both elementary and high schools."

I encouraged him, "Tell me more, Johnny."

"I went to high school for six years because that is all I could be funded for. I learned glasswork." I had not heard of that as a subject before, so I continued to probe him for more information.

He explained that he was trained in doing mosaics with glass. That was as far as I got with Johnny because customers were entering the store.

I seated myself next to Daisy when another one of the people that she helped journey through difficult times, came into the store. Her name is Vicki and she was in a very serious car accident that left her in a coma for months. She suffered resultant brain damage, lost one eye, and has had expensive plastic surgery. Daisy whispered into my ear, "She has a tendency to perseverate and interrupt. She also loves clothes and usually dresses with flair."

I witnessed Daisy being kind but firm with her.

"Daisy, Daisy, I will give you a dollar for these two things. Please, Daisy." She was pleading because she knew that the officials at the group home had complained to Daisy that she hoarded clothes.

"They are everywhere and she does not hang anything," Daisy whispered to me.

"No, Vicki, you can only take one thing. You know the rules." Daisy spoke firmly.

Vicki went on, "But Daisy, I need these pants and I want to give my sister the sweater for Christmas," she was manipulating.

"No, Vicki," Daisy replied. "Only one thing and put the other back where you got it."

"But Daisy, I want to take it to show my sister now to see if she likes it. Please, Daisy, please." I can still hear the chant. Daisy conceded to let her give it a try with her sister but she wanted her to bring something back in exchange for what she was taking.

"But Daisy, I will pay you a dollar. Please, Daisy! Oh please!"

Daisy stayed firm, "You heard me, Vicki. You can take one thing for you, another for your sister to try, but you must bring something back in return."

"I will, Daisy, I will. Oh thank you, Daisy. I love you, Daisy. I love you, Daisy," she went on.

"I love you too. Go now!" Daisy ruled and she left.

I witnessed Daisy being comfortable with her fierceness, as well as her generosity in terms of setting limits with Vicki who had no understanding of what was enough. This, I have come to believe, is a very important aspect of mature feminine development.

13

> "I picked up the wounds while they
> wandered around sleepwalking."
>
> Sandra C. Johnston

When I went to Daisy's today, Jane, one of Daisy's helpers from the Lodge was waiting in a chair again for Daisy to give her directions. Daisy directed her to vacuum the upper floor and she went off to do the job.

A young man in his early twenties who Daisy introduced to me as Bill came into inquire about the watches that Daisy had promised to bring to the store for him to appraise. Bill told Daisy that he was prepared to pay $3.00 for those he chose and Daisy remained firm about the $5.00 price. She told him that she would have the watches for him early the following week. We must not forget that Daisy has to bring in at least $40.00 a day in order to pay the rent.

Jane had finished the vacuuming and Daisy told her to sit for a while.

I could not help but watch Jane. I have a tendency to do that because I have been a therapist for so long. She sat with her eyes rolled back in their sockets completely dissociated from us. When Daisy or I tried to bring her into the conversation though, she was lucid enough to give us short answers. She looked depressed and seemed to have very little motivation. I wondered how much medication she was on.

I was getting a clearer sense of what Daisy has had to do over the years and how much she has seen in terms of mistreatment of those who came into her mentorship. I felt sad and angry at the same time. So many of them had been robotized and duped by a system that speaks about appropriate care for the disabled and mentally challenged.

Daisy referred to her experience with the hearing aid specialist the day before. She shared that she felt the specialist watching her in a patronizing way when she attempted to put her own hearing aids in.

"Why is it that so many who see an older woman think that they can't do anything for themselves and move to help when they are not being asked to?"

I wondered if she was remarking that it seems that when women come into their later years, others believed that they needed to be treated as invalids. I have hypothesized many times that an unconscious need exists in the collective to render them 'in-valid'. In my experience, that pattern has become entrenched because fear and a lack of authentic curiosity are extant in our culture. Devaluation is certainly a way to render someone speechless and powerless.

Was Daisy identifying with those she helped?

I know that I have lived with that kind of compassion, but the dark forces are dense in this politic now and they have been for too long. It is difficult for anyone to live with that kind of sensitivity but neither Daisy nor I have given up like so many have. Perhaps that is why we met each other in this lifetime. She has made a difference in her community, and so have I. We had both chosen to create an underground in the best way we knew how, so that we could expose the dysfunctional and attempt to create an awareness of a need for change.

Bill came in to assess Daisy's watches and told her to put a few aside that were worth more than $5.00. She directed me to find a basket for them to display and to make a sign that put them on special for $5.00 a watch. While I was helping her arrange the watches, she commented, "I have come to know know Bill over time, and he is such a fine young man."

Kirsten, who was Betty's worker, came into the store shortly after Bill exited. She looked very tired. After finding a few pieces of clothing for herself, she asked Daisy and I if we might be able to stay open a little later that day because she wanted to introduce her adolescent daughter to the store and to Daisy and me. We stayed open long enough to have them come back. We met a very competent daughter with a very competent mother who was admitting that she was on the edge of burnout working in the system.

"I see so much political nonsense every day, and I feel so helpless to change things for those in my care," Kirsten sighed.

She told us that her daughter was president of her student council and very much into environmental issues. As the conversation went on, it was very obvious that the daughter needed her mother to change. The pain for many daughters is that they want their mothers to free them but they end up trying to free their mothers.

"My daughter is helping me with this rescue thing," Kirsten shared.

Her daughter looked straight at me, "I hope that she will get it."

Kirsten had lamented earlier about how work identified she was because of the women in her Portuguese past who knew only servitude. Are daughters asking their mothers to 'get a life' so that they can have one?

I have come to the awareness myself that this all has to do with learning to value and love oneself as a woman before one can move to truly love, share with, and help others. We all need a balance of work, love, and play.

Mother and daughter left the store and Daisy and I prepared for closing just as Patty came to drive her mother home.

Daisy refreshed her lipstick and put on her leopard style vest. I could not help but be enthralled by her beauty and light, both inside and outside. She started to tell me about her brother and her son who had special needs. She mentioned that her son had passed away and she started to cry. I moved to hold her then. *I knew that her tears were the germination of what has preserved her. They purified the wounds that she has suffered. A very pure hearted woman cried these tears. They were holy water.*

For women, tears are the initiation into the clan of the "Scarred Ones" and not the scared ones. We are a timeless tribe of women of all colors, all nations, and all languages who down through the ages have come through a great something and yet stood proud. There are oceans of tears women have not cried because they have been trained to carry mother's and father's secrets, men's secrets and their own to the grave. A woman's crying has been seen as quite dangerous because great winds will begin to create force gales. She will howl and scream when she unbolts the door to the closet containing corpses of the dead feminine and she will never run away or hide again. Secrets will be shared and naiveté and powerlessness will be transformed into active and creative self-responsibility.

I locked up the store for Daisy and my heart felt both opened and softened by all that happened that day.

14

> "The most honest thing I can do as an artist is to disturb and blow some of the sacred myths apart. I must be prepared to be an outcast."
>
> *Sandra C. Johnston*

When I entered Daisy's store today Donald, (who Daisy refers to as the mountain man because of his beard and his height) was sitting on the fourth step leading up to the kitchen wares. He was wearing a suit and tie. He always comes dressed that way because Daisy prefers that he looks presentable at all times. A customer had brought in a bagful of her husband's old clothes and Daisy wanted them to be put onto hangers and hung on the appropriate racks. She directed Donald to sit by her and place the shirts on hangers and hand them to me so I could put them in their proper location. The lady who had brought the donations decided to look around the store.

I asked Donald where he lived and he answered, "I live in a dump of a group home." I couldn't help but laugh at the comment and asked him to tell me more.

"Well," he said, "the place is really falling apart and I sleep on a single mattress with holes in it. The lady in charge has a big bed upstairs."

Daisy entered the conversation then and Donald went on to explain to the two of us that, "the furniture is very old, the couch has holes in it. There is a board under the cushions to support them evenly and the bathrooms have never been renovated since the place was built many years ago."

The lady who had been browsing put the scarf that she had been wearing around her neck with intent to purchase, back on the rack. She said, "I have to leave because it all seems so Dickensian here." She exited then.

Donald is an oppressed man and yes, there are some in the culture. He lives on the fringes of society and he has been marginalized. He feels helpless to do anything about his situation. Perhaps this woman was feeling as depressed as he was and could not handle listening to truth.

I taught high school English in my early twenties and Dickens' novel, "Hard Times" was on the curriculum. I was too young to grasp a great deal of what he was trying to expose in his works, but I have come to understand his concerns over time. He spoke to the issues of the lost, the oppressed and the bewildered child. He had contempt for law and parliament and his writings were characterized by attacks on social evils and inadequate institutions. He always maintained a spirit of benevolence and generosity. I have witnessed this knowing, this kindness and generosity attributed to Charles Dickens in Daisy Walls.

The woman, who left the store in a hurry like many of us, would rather not experience or know the truth of the conditions of a facility in her own town.

She reminds me of so many who feel safer turning a blind eye to the conditions that exist outside their environments if they are safe at all. This denial only serves to perpetuate the crimes that continue to take place against the disenfranchised, be they women, some men, children, minority groups, the handicapped or special needs people.

Daisy had Donald clean the front door window and then he took his leave having put in his time to receive $20.00 from the government. This gives him some weekly spending money along with his paper route.

It was time to close again and Daisy was on her way to have her hearing aids checked. I would not have known that she wore them because they are small and she never seems to miss anything auditory.

I decided to treat myself to a coffee at the coffee shop just across the road from the store and I met Donald sitting in a corner having his coffee. I acknowledged him and he smiled. I stopped at the variety store down the street after that. I usually drop in to say, "Hello" to the owners. The male owner commented ironically, "Well, you have certainly chosen to work in one of the most depressing places in White Rock." I was taken aback by the comment and then he continued. "I don't know but I just did not like the energy in there. It was like something from a Dickens novel." He reminded me of my partner who had made similar comments to me, insinuating that I was working in a crazy house.

I responded somewhat defensively. "The people who work for Daisy are the fringe people and it saddens me that we automatically feel fear when someone is different in terms of looks, speech demeanor and attire. We have not been taught much patience or openness." I had to be careful not to let myself get into a diatribe because I was feeling angry.

While I was riding the elevator to my living quarters, I remembered having read a novel by John Windham called "The Chrysalids." I felt a great deal of sadness when I taught it because of the prejudice he exposed about our culture's tendency to make outcasts out of those who do not appear normal or to live normally.

I ask now, "What is normal? Is it just that everyone does certain things according to a script, even if it is not working?" I believe I am speaking about the tendency to live according to the 'pathological' norm. This has lead to the black and white thinking that is endemic to and epidemic in our addictive society.

It has not been by accident that the one eyed and the lame or those with withered limbs or other physical and mental differences, have been sought out as possessing special knowing. The injuries or the differences force these people early on into a different kind of seeing.

I believe that who and what we have been taught to fear might have a great deal to teach us.

Daisy has provided many of these people with a safe place to come to and feel good about themselves in community. For the most part as I have personally witnessed, many of them are not able to self-initiate. Daisy has been and still is in the position of mentoring and directing them. Her store is a creative place and not sanitized in the sense that she is not so worried about standards as she is about serving those in need and giving them a chance to feel some competency in their world.

There are many stories, fairy tales, and myths about abandoned and crippled children who are welcomed by 'elder' people. They nurse the child back to health and help the child find extraordinary power. I feel more dedicated to helping Daisy while I write this book more than ever now. In time, I will come to know why I landed in White Rock. I believed that I was seeking a 'place' of higher consciousness when I left Ontario. I have come to know that wherever I go, there I am.

The question for me now is "What will I be like after these experiences?" I am choosing to live into the answers, however difficult the process might be for me. I have heard the statement and I paraphrase, "Any fool can run towards the light, but it takes a master with courage to turn and face the darkness and chose to move into the light."

15

> "A woman's life can really be a succession of lives, each revolving around some emotionally compelling situation of challenge and each marked off by some intense experience."
>
> *Wallis Simpson*

Daisy and I had a few minutes together before we opened the store. I asked her to tell me more about her experience with Marilyn Monroe. She smiled broadly as she began to tell me the story.

"My husband was working in Jasper at the time and he called me to come there. Marilyn was to be boarding the train at three o'clock; she was leaving the set. I got there and she was with a haughty British woman whose name was Natasha. In her protectiveness or whatever the hell she was doing, she informed me that Marilyn was tired and did not want to give autographs. Marilyn turned to Natasha and told her in no uncertain terms, 'This lady is the only one who came to see me and I would love to sign my autograph for her'."

I went with my second daughter afterwards to see the lodge cabins where she stayed. She had been filming with Robert Mitchum and Rory Calhoun. Their wives went to the same restaurant that my daughter and I frequented when we went to Jasper. We met them, talked with them, and took pictures of them. Marilyn died in 1963, and I felt that I was losing a friend because of that special moment I shared with her. She was more beautiful in real life than in the movies. She wore a black sweater with sleeves and light colored jeans. It looked as though she would have had to grease her body in order to squeeze into them! But she possessed a beautiful spirit. It is too bad she got mixed up with the Kennedys. The night that she sang 'Happy Birthday' for John Kennedy, she was pinned into her dress and drunk. Her story was mostly about boys having sex with her and men having used her. She was a heart broken woman. When she was married to Joe Di Maggio, she was in Japan and people were falling all over her. He was a very jealous man, of course, and he was upset when she stole the limelight. No one even recognized Joe. That was the kind of charisma Marilyn had. When the wind blew her dress up, he was devastated and angry. Then she married Arthur Miller who was 'stuck in his mind' and she couldn't handle him."

A customer came into the store at that point and Daisy moved to wait on her. *I just sat in reverie for a while picturing Marilyn embracing Daisy. I was considering how instinct wounded many women are, especially when they have been wounded in the feminine body early in life. They lack the instinct to recognize the traps, to know when that is enough, to create boundaries around health and welfare, to understand that excesses break and weaken us until we become a puddle instead of a powerful force. Perhaps Marilyn could have thrived with a wise woman like Daisy. She needed someone she could hold onto, until she could hold on to one shred of instinct that would last until she could begin the time-consuming work of rebuilding inner sense and instinct. Male rescuers and users coming down the pike when she was most vulnerable were not the answer to her female dilemma. I could personally and painfully identify with her.*

Daisy does not want me to leave White Rock and she has said so many times. She possesses high instinct and I hear her whisper…"Stay here long enough Sandra …long enough to revive your hope, to give up defensive half truths… long enough to see what is right for you, long enough to get strong, to try the try that will make it. Stay here long enough to make it to the finish line no matter how long it takes or in what style."

Daisy has given me a reason to stay here or I would have packed my bags to go, long ago. Never given room to thrive is hard on a woman's vitality and I have to surrender pretence as I begin to walk the path of writing again. Life is deadly without a confidant, a guide, and a cheering section. I will start to live in the open now as I see fit and leave deep footprints wherever I can. The water of this story will not only be deep, but clear.

Will there be a striking revision of the old me?

Finished

*Never again will I wear
The mask
That covered the lies
That gave order to that
Onerous task of uncovering!*

16

> "Creative art is a learning process for the artist and not a description of what is already known…the work needs concentration and one is often exhausted by it…"
>
> *Gertrude Stein*

Johnny was counting pennies again when I arrived to assist Daisy. I did not see her right away; when I asked him where she was, he said, "Vicki is here and she is getting on Daisy's nerves and mine too." I was concerned and thought that Daisy might be in the bathroom when she suddenly appeared around the corner from the clothing section. She did not have to say anything because her face showed it all; she looked tired and frustrated to me.

Vicki was there to put in her two hours of service, as she does every Friday. Her ritual had become one of scouting out the goods before she started to dust. She was looking somewhat crazed and began to harass Daisy for items of clothing she really did not need. She tested Daisy's patience over and over again. Soon, I was feeling angry.

So many women are taught in the socialization process 'to normalize the abnormal' and to 'make nice so many atrocities'. Just because this young woman was brain damaged and probably suffered from psychosis, it should not be a case for Daisy to have to handle at this stage of her life. I began to wonder then about Daisy's high toleration for this level of personal frustration. Was she trained early to miss her own pain and focus on the pain of others? It was a question I began to formulate, now knowing I would experience the answers over time. It was a mystery.

Daisy told Vicki to put several pieces of clothing back where they belonged. Vicki had already put three items aside and I missed that scenario because it took place before I arrived. I took the coveted clothes out of her hands and put them back on the rack. I had to be very firm with her and she stopped for a short time.

"You must stop this now, Vicki," I reprimanded. She started to dust and found more things to covet. She began to hassle Daisy again. It was like watching an addict screaming for a fix.

Daisy told her to leave and she turned to Daisy trying to hug her saying, "I am so sorry, Daisy, I am so sorry, Daisy. Please, Daisy. I am so sorry, Daisy." I listened to the emptiness in her voice anguished and helpless. No empathy could be sufficient.

Daisy said, "You are not sorry because you keep doing the same thing over and over! You can go home now." I felt relieved.

Daisy offered to rub my hands and I told her that I should be rubbing hers. "I don't have arthritis and you do, so sit."

We were seated side by side when a man introduced to me as Grant, came in the door. He had known Daisy for several years and it was evident that she had mentored him over time. He had his lunch with him and offered to share some with Daisy. Lunch consisted of chocolate bars, potato chips, soda crackers and two cans of pop. Daisy very graciously declined and he sat close to her. She quietly spoke to me as he organized his lunch. "He has been in rehabilitation for alcohol abuse and is presently living with his parents."

He engaged her with the question, "What was your first job, Daisy?"

She quickly shared that she did housecleaning and looked after a little boy. "I was fifteen years old and I made $5.00 a month. I bought my first skirt from a bargain shop."

"What color was it, Daisy?" Grant inquired.

"It was pale blue and the next month I found my way into Vancouver by streetcar and went straight to the Hudson Bay Company. The store had a bargain basement and I found a jacket that was an exact match to the skirt. I had just enough money to get back home on the streetcar."

"Tell me about your first job, Grant," Daisy became curious.

"I was thirteen and I sold Christmas trees. I wanted to blend in and find some friends."

I felt sad then because I was aware of the loneliness that he must have felt then and my instinctual perception of him was that he still feels it. He called Daisy, "Doll", and seemed so appreciative of her. He lingered for a while when other customers started to come into the store and then took his leave offering me two small chocolate bars. I had a sense that he had been in search of some emotional nurturance that he was used to getting from Daisy.

It was time to change the Remembrance Day window and Daisy directed me to the pajama section to get the best of the nightwear. In the process of trying to locate the appropriate hangers, I felt that I was outside of my comfort zone. I have never had to do window displays and I was distracted at that moment by a woman who wanted a blanket to take to her niece's cottage. I felt the pressure of time because I had to be at my doctor's at a certain time. The woman wanted to chat and told me that she was originally from Ontario. I told her where I came from and she wanted to share her experiences in that neck of the woods! What with the window, finding the pajamas, the right hangers, talking to the customer and needing to leave, I was feeling overwhelmed. I had to make a quick exit, promising Daisy that I would return to complete the window display.

I was longer than I expected at the doctor's office and when I returned, Daisy had already called Patty and told her that I would give her a ride home. Vicki came back to the store right at closing time and demanded that Daisy sell her the three items she had put away at the start of the day. Daisy and I were somewhat 'out of joint' by then and the two of us had to deal with Vicki's self anxiety, her need for a clothes fix, her manipulation, and her constant interruption.

Daisy charged her appropriately for the clothing but Vicki said, "Daisy, this is crazy! I should have a discount because I work in the store."

This decision was Daisy's way of trying to get Vicki to be more accountable, in terms of the boarding home officials' concerns about her clothes hoarding. She was upset with Daisy but paid the required amount. She had $7.00 left and she was adamant now that she needed to buy a broach for her stepmother.

This had become her ruse in that if she could not buy it for herself then somebody else needed it whether it was her mother, her dad, her stepmother, her sister or, some friend!

Daisy very firmly said, "No, Vicki, not until tomorrow!"

Vicki kept on insisting even to the point of asking for a belt buckle. Daisy told her to leave in no uncertain terms then, and I turned out the lights.

Daisy turned to me and said, "I think I am ready for the insane asylum." I looked at her and said, "Me too!"

I was still not sure of my way around White Rock but Daisy was so understanding that she had the patience not only to direct me to her house but she had me make a full circle around her subdivision so that I could find my way back home. I am always amazed at the compassion and patience that Daisy possesses, and I felt grateful once again to have been in her presence that day.

I did have to take a long nap when I arrived home because I was out of energy and I wondered how Daisy was faring.

17

"The writer must be a psychologist, but a secret one: he/she must sense and know the roots of phenomena, but offer only the phenomena themselves, as they blossom or whither."

Ivan Turgenev

Just as I suspected from the scenario the day before, Vicki was at the door waiting for Daisy to arrive. I saw her outside from my window. She wanted to return the items that she bought the night before. Daisy gave her the money back. I wondered what it might be like to have a 'no return policy' or to inform the officials in charge that Vicki was not suitable for the job, that she made customers go away, and that she was abusive as well as manipulative. I ask, "What stops us? Is it guilt or pity and who is harming whom?"

It is obvious that Vicki does not understand her effect upon others and probably never will. So do we become like them and operate at their level, or do we recognize our own limits and what it costs us physically, emotionally, mentally and spiritually? What stops us from setting the limits and becoming more concerned with self-care? Are there not facilities that specialize in caring for those with this level of disturbance? Why am I feeling so angry?

Johnny had shared that all of the residents at the group home are disturbed by Vicki's behaviors and her presence in general.

This aggression, rage, frustration, and inappropriate behaviors are projected out onto everyone who will contain them, and the victim may end up feeling like a perpetrator, not realizing the set-up. It is difficult to try to manage another's internal states, and the trauma of dealing with them has to do with trying to make sense of someone's unstable perceptions. I felt nauseous.

I am over my head with Vicki and I believe that Daisy is also, even though she says that she can let it go once she gets home. I wondered if she might have to brace herself constantly for the next onslaught. It feels like walking on eggshells when Vicki is around. I have personal experience with trauma and the therapist. I have been forced, over time, to know what my limits are and what I can deal with realistically, given what I now accept as the nature of my own personal sensibilities. I am not sure at this point that I am much different from Daisy in terms of these sensitivities given my direct experience of her. I could not help but wonder how honest she was being with herself, or how honest I was being with myself at this point in time.

In the earlier Matristic cultures that existed before Patriarchy was entrenched, elder women were given high status as advisors and mentors. They presided over communities and councils. The difficult work was relegated to initiates in training so they could help others to handle life's passages. I could not help but formulate the question "Isn't this where Daisy should be now?"

I can see her on the throne of the high priestess summoning council in order to generate new ideas and to preserve the legacy of all that she has learned and accomplished through trial and error. Instead, she has Rick and Robert focusing on the throne in the bathroom.

Grant dropped in again today and put a watch on lay-away. I know that he came in to see Daisy again and experience connection. He said, "Goodbye, Doll," when he was leaving. He was speaking to her in terms of endearment once again. He will be back soon because he needs warmth, a sense of spirit and connection to help him stay sober. I am not sure this will be enough to sustain him in terms of his real and perceived abandonment issues. He is one of many attempting to concretize spirit through the use of 'spirits', food, sex, power, drugs, or relationships.

Neva who had been working for Daisy for a few years came in to work today; she and I had a good time finishing the pajama window. I was relieved to have her help me because I knew nothing about the special hangers and how to prop them. We put some artificial flowers in a small make-up suitcase to support one set of the sleepwear and found some perfume bottles to enhance the display. I must say that it looked good, and Daisy was pleased. I thoroughly enjoyed Neva's humor and level of personal awareness. We enjoyed bantering with one another.

Another lady came in with her daughter looking for dolls. I was not sure about the extent of Daisy's doll collection, but I soon had to learn. Daisy and Neva were busy with other customers and so I was doing solo. One of the dolls behind the counter was a walking doll and when I lifted her out, the head came off! The lady remarked, "Someone has put the wrong head on the doll and so the head does not flow into the neck." It hung to the left in a lop-sided manner!

There were several dolls behind glass in the cupboard behind the counter. I had never looked in there before and so I pulled out every doll to show the customer. I must say that we both had some fun looking at some of these wounded girls. Some were lacking arms, others lacked legs, some were parched from the sun, some were naked, and some only partially clothed.

I am still not sure what Daisy was intending in terms of keeping them and I was a little afraid to ask. All of these broken dolls around made me curious. Daisy noticed what we were doing and sent me to the dressing room to fetch a doll behind the curtain in there. I was frightened when I located it because she had a big baldhead connected to the chest with adhesive tape. She was missing her right arm and all that was left of it was a wire. The lady made no comment about the state of the doll but she quickly bought a tiny little doll from the front cabinet and left.

Daisy instructed me to place the two hideous refugees on the chair near the front door. I felt that I would probably find a better place for them over time in case they frightened the customers when they entered the store. They certainly were frightening looking to me and not very loveable.

I had an experience with dolls and doll parts when I was in graduate school doing my internship. I had rented a room from a colleague who I did not know very well. I was still very naïve in the world even at forty- two years of age. I was a woman without her instincts intact at that point in time. There was a room just outside of my bedroom that was always closed. I hesitantly asked landlady-colleague to show me what was in there. She opened the door and over one hundred dolls stood looking at me with big glass eyes that seemed to follow me around. I was freaked! I was never comfortable in that house after that. She had doll moulds and doll parts throughout her basement too, and I made sure that I never did my laundry there.

I am not a doll lover anymore, especially of broken dolls. I have heard that dolls are a reflection of our inner states. This lady was stuck in her injuries from early childhood. I left her place and chose never to see her again. I guess I was bringing death to something without full knowledge.

18

"I cannot give you the formula for success, but I can give you the formula for failure: try to please everybody."

Herbert Bayard Swope

I had to go to the dentist's office today for a cleaning. While I was with the hygienist she asked me what I was writing and so I explained that I was writing about Daisy Walls, a ninety-one year old woman who was as bright as a silver dollar. My mouth was full of instruments and running water and she began to tell me about her elder aunt, her grandmother's sister who was dissident in terms of her family's definition of her. The young woman laughed then and told me, "The last time I saw my aunt was at a family gathering and she had seated herself at the end of the couch. After she finished her meal, she looked around sheepishly and stuffed her dirty napkin under the pillows on the couch." I nearly choked because of the visual picture that I had of her aunt. The young woman took the instruments out so that I could finish laughing. She put them back in again and told me that her Granny had Alzheimer's disease. She seemed to want to share her story and she had a captive listener!

"At the last party that my family had, Granny was sitting close to the cake and I ended up giving her four pieces of the dessert. Granny leaned over to me and said, "They all think I have forgotten that I have had so many pieces but let them think that. I love cake and I don't worry about my figure anymore." I almost choked again on the instruments and had to be relieved of their burden in order to laugh out loud. The two of us were having a great time now.

She replaced the instruments and told me, "I have always been interested in psychology and so I took a course on Women's Issues. I was required to do a paper on older women and had thirty days within which to complete it. I slacked off and had to come up with something so I made stories up about Granny so that I could please the professor and I received an excellent mark. The assignment had to do with developmental theory and so I slotted Granny into the stages with tales that were not true. I felt so guilty. Then Granny wanted to read my paper and I had to change it all so that it reflected the truth of my real experiences with Granny and she loved it."

My session was over and I had to leave and get ready for the afternoon with Daisy. I thanked the young woman for sharing her stories with me and I left the dental office felling relieved that this young woman was learning to think outside the box when she recognized her reflex to define her Granny in a certain way to placate her professor. My hope is that my granddaughter will rely on her direct experiences of me and not upon anyone else's definition of me.

When I arrived at Daisy's she had a table out to create a jewelry display. She had five bags of jewelry donated that morning and she had been planning a before-Christmas sale anyway. She sent me behind the jewelry counter to start sorting and I found it overwhelming. I laid two bags on the top of the counter and began to sort the bracelets from the earrings, the chains from the necklaces and to undo all kinds of knots in the chains that had wound around one another. I knew that I had my job set out for me the next day as well. I thought that this project might be something that Betty could help me with.

Rick came in at that point to fix the clock and then there was a rush of customers because it was '$1.49 Tuesday' again. He left because of the confusion and returned with a coffee for me before he took his walk to the ocean. I was getting a sense that he was beginning to rely on me for some quick answers to his existential questions and some soothing. I made a mental note of it. I would not allow him to rely on me or to cling to me.

Daisy's daughter, Wendie, came to pick Daisy up to take her to the hairdresser and the day was complete in terms of the store. Wendie asked Daisy about the 'for sale' sign on the building because she thought that the present owners were renovating. Daisy said, "No, they are selling it and that will mean I will retire."

I exclaimed, "Daisy, you will be signing books!"

"Yes!" she responded and added, "I will be sending one to Oprah!"

19

> "Silence is not just a product but a major source of fear, which also explains why it impedes the recovery of those who have been traumatized."
>
> *Eviator Zerabavel*

On this windy, dark, and cold November day I made my way over to Daisy's. I thought that because of the inclement weather that there might be only a few customers. I wanted more time with Daisy alone in order to get more facts about her life. It did not seem to go that way though, and I find it interesting how the story is winding its own way toward some kind of finish line. There is mystery here and I have to remind myself that this opus is process oriented and not goal oriented. I catch myself having to remind myself to honor feminine values and to practice what I preach.

When I arrived in the store, Daisy was sitting with Stacey and Winnie. I had forgotten that they came in to help on Sundays. The three of them seemed to be enjoying themselves chatting and I joined the circle. Winnie reiterated that she would not be with us if it hadn't been for Daisy. She had made reference to that fact the previous Sunday. Her story this day was about her depressive episodes, the hospitalizations, and the group homes that she had experienced over a number of years.

"I was picked up in a ditch, with my orange bird, by strangers when I was trying to get away from a particular group home where

I felt isolated and helpless. The couple drove me to the hospital where I stayed for three weeks before I was sent back to the same group home. I tried to jump off of the pier into the Pacific Ocean after that, and a man jumped into the water and pulled me out. I was hospitalized on the psychiatric ward, once again, but this time they heard me and I did not have to return to that group home."

I reframed, "You were crying for help, Winnie."

"Yes, I felt powerless and helpless. My parents had passed away and my brothers had entered the military; I had no one to talk to."

"I feel so sad, Winnie," I was validating her feelings. "You must have felt so lonely."

I had traveled that same road too but not at the level that Winnie had. I had felt the extreme isolation, capture and lived without a hearing many times in my life. I am left to wonder, as I write, about how many women have truly felt the same feelings but felt compelled to hide their distress, because they felt shame for experiencing it. This is where the 'conspiracy of silence' became an enforced mandate for women, children, and minority groups. When issues of abuse, (physically, emotionally and psychologically) including incest and rape came up, they were kept secret and went underground. These subordinates in a white male dominant culture were taught to keep the secrets of men out of fear of more abuse. There is still a clandestine inquisition operating today in my opinion, based on personal and professional experience.

Winnie continued, "I went to Daisy's after she set up her store and services and she helped me to gain a sense of hope. Eventually, I was able to take my life back again." She had met Daisy at a crossroad in her life, just as I had.

Stacey sat quietly throughout the conversation with Winnie. She seemed very vigilant. I began to speak directly to her and I sensed then that she had been taught to speak only when spoken to. She didn't seem comfortable with taking her space in the circle, the conversation, and perhaps the world. While Stacey was putting on her coat to get ready to leave Daisy whispered, "She came to the store for months and months and never uttered a word."

Daisy looked straight at her now and said, "Sandra, Stacey has a job at the Party Bazaar in Vancouver." Stacey's eyes lit up and she nodded affirmatively with a broad smile.

"How do you get to work, Stacey?" I inquired out of genuine interest.

"I take the skytrain into Vancouver," she replied.

I had an image in my mind's eye then of Daisy getting on the streetcar when she was fifteen with her first pay. She was on her way to the bargain basement of the Hudson's Bay Company.

Daisy offered, "Stacey's sister manages the Party Bazaar."

"What department do you work in Stacey?" I was curious and I wanted to get to know her better because I had a sense that she might be quite bright.

She answered me, "I work in the warehouse where I price things and I like it very much."

"Good for you," I complimented her.

Stacey took her leave and Rick entered. We had not seen him for a few days. He seemed apologetic and flustered when he told us that he had been busy driving some of his new friends around.

"What's up, Rick?" I asked.

"Well, now my shower head is completely broken and I have found out from the plumbing store that it is obsolete and very difficult to replace." He had mentioned days earlier that the landlords were away and that he was left in charge of any maintenance that had to be done on the building, which included Daisy's store.

"I have spent the whole morning trying to fix it and paint the ceiling as well. Then unexpected company came and lingered."

"So you are feeling frustrated, Rick," I witnessed the look of despair on his face.

"No, not really," he claimed.

Daisy took her turn to speak. "Rick, I have been noticing

that you have not been tending to your whiskers and beard." Rick bowed his head towards his chest at that point.

"It is a sign of neglecting yourself and focusing on others, Rick. I notice that you are not yourself." Daisy continued, "You must watch that you do not give yourself away to rinky-dinks."

I laughed out loud!

Rick retorted sheepishly, "I could never tell those people that or I would put a dint in their day."

I could not help myself and blurted, "So, they would not like to hear the truth of your experience of them. Is that what you are trying to tell us, Rick?" *I liked to stir him up sometimes and force him to do some intrapsychic sorting. I was forgetting that I was not his therapist and I was losing a sense of my boundaries in spite of my intention not to.*

He went on to justify his behavior, "There are a whole bunch of us in White Rock of similar age and we all seem to be in some sort of transition."

"You mean lost?" I queried.

"Well," he started, "one of the women has divorced and her son went out to live on his own. She has never been alone before and is experiencing the empty nest syndrome. The other friend is here from Germany away from his family. He has been here for nearly a year. He has to legitimize his reasons for staying here in Canada or, his wife will think that he is schmoozing and having affairs."

I was hesitant to comment but I did, "That is not your problem, Rick."

Daisy interjected, "We all have a higher power, Rick, and we should not need rescuers."

"What is that supposed to mean, Daisy?" He was becoming more defensive.

"Well, Rick," she said, "You need to join the club of those who are choosing to live more consciously on a day to day basis, willing to keep learning about their behavior, how it affects others, and questioning over and over again where our responsibilities lie.

Life is a mystery and I believe that our task is to find out the good things that we are meant to do personally by really listening and paying attention. This does not always mean helping those who are perfectly capable of helping themselves, especially given your energy and resources."

"You know, Daisy, that I always listen to what you have to say and deliberately seek your wisdom. I understand where you are coming from today, but I do need to tell you that my way is to have direct experience in order to learn these things. I do feel that people like you show up in my life to help me on my way." He was expressing ambivalence and hostility with a smile on his face.

I thought of the bumbling knight, Parsifal, who had to stumble into enlightenment and formulate the question, "What ails thee?" to the depressed King of a kingdom that had become a wasteland. The questions came up for Parsifal and he had to live into the answers. He was in search of the Holy Grail and would eventually have to ask, "Whom does the Grail serve?" Ultimately, the answer had to do with altruism and serving humankind without hidden agendas.

I wanted to believe that Rick was becoming more aware of his learning style and beginning to ask important existential questions that come with age. He seemed, to me, to be living out the archetype of the Knight who was desirous of a sense of true belonging. He left us, I believe, with some sense of relief. Neither Daisy nor I were interested in supporting his illusions, or should I say, delusions! I believe as well, that we were becoming 'hooked in' despite our intentions not to be and might end up end up losing energy to Rick ourselves. Sometimes the very thing we teach we have most to learn.

Bill came into the store just after Rick's leave taking. He had promised Daisy earlier in the week that he would come back to assess some watches that she promised to bring in from her home. He found two watches that were collectors' items but mentioned that they were not in good shape. He also found an old Bulova that needed some repair. He and Daisy always do some dickering. Bill offered her $20.00 for one of the most valuable of the three, $8.00 for the other and $5.00 for the Bulova. He offered the eight dollars for one of the watches that day and he promised that he would come the next day to pay for the others.

"You are always as good as your word, Bill, and that is alright with me," Daisy smiled at him.

"The two Gucci watches are fake and the others are good for the $5.00 basket on the counter," he added.

Daisy was satisfied with the deal that she and Bill had made together because it meant that she would almost make the rent that day.

Bill left and Daisy wanted me to make sure that I referenced him in the book because he was such a fine young man. "When he first came to White Rock, he was like a hippie and somewhat bedraggled. Over the past couple of years he has worked very hard trying to become a self made man. He has made it up the ranks in the restaurant industry and he has become an excellent cook. He seems very responsible and I have had the pleasure of watching him grow up."

"What a rewarding experience, Daisy," I concurred with her assessment of Bill's character from my own experience of him since I came to be with Daisy.

It was closing time once again and we turned out the lights on a very good note once again.

20

"Breaking the silence is a moral act par excellence."
Martin Luther King

It is Wednesday evening and I am burning the midnight oils. I had to take a nap after being at the store today because I was feeling exhausted. Of course, sleeping in the afternoon meant that I would be up late and so, here I sit at the computer. I tried to sleep twice but I could not sink into it because of some of the events of the day were still fresh in my mind. I can usually deal with my busy mind through yoga and meditation but practice was not working for me tonight. I felt that a de-briefing was in order, so I decided that it was best to write things down and ground myself.

Garth, the man who came in my life, does not like what I am doing in the store because he thinks it is a crazy house, and he hates the fact that I have to write in the evening. I am left often to deal with daily events in my mind or write them down. I believe in what I am doing and that is all that matters to me in this space in time. It would be wonderful to experience a cheering section! I cannot help but feel the conflict within me when I sit long enough to wonder whether I can trust my own perceptions or whether he is seeing things more clearly than I am.

Betty had come to the store soon after I arrived at the door today; she was full of excitement about working with me.

"I think that I look like a Hollywood star today because of the way I am dressed. Don't you think so, Sandra?"

"You do look very pretty today, Betty," I concurred.

"We have some work ahead of us today in terms of sorting the jewelry table." I wanted to give her some focus right away.

I arranged several boxes for us to sort and pair earrings up. She took the chair beside me and we began the operation. She found a gold plated heart shaped broach that she said that her mother would like. I told her to put it aside and that she could pay Daisy when she came to work the following week. She was elated to have found something for her mother. She began to open up to me and to tell me some of her life story. I assumed that she was feeling safe with me.

"You know how I came to be here at the lodge don't you?" she started.

"No, I don't," I replied.

"Well you see, I lived in Toronto and in my early twenties I was walking down the street when I saw a man that looked like a mobster staring at me. I felt hypnotized by him and I could not move. The next thing I knew, he grabbed me and took me into an alley where he made me have sex with another man while he watched. The other man then stuck a broom handle into me and they left me in the alley bleeding. I got dressed and walked further down the street and I saw a police station, but I could not speak when I entered. I remember asking them for a cigarette and nothing more."

I sat uncomfortably in my chair feeling horrified and angry. "You were raped, Betty." My throat felt constricted. I wanted to scream.

She rebuffed me and said, "I don't like that word and he was clean. I don't think that he had any diseases."

This woman, now so wounded in her body and instincts, was 'making nice' of the most horrible atrocities! While she was confused, the men raped her. She was so unbalanced she complied with their orders.

I felt uneasy when a customer entered the store, and the conversation came to an end for the time being.

Betty asked me, "Would it be be all right if I step outside for a couple of puffs of a cigarette?" I told her to go right ahead. This was her way of narcotizing her pain; I could have used one too!

The customer left and Betty took her seat beside me once again to continue sorting, and she began to add to her story.

"I want to tell you some other things, Sandra. Another time a man dragged me into a place where two prostitutes and I were told to undress and he started to bite my breasts. I had to be hospitalized then and I have never been the same since. When I got into the hospital, a nasty nurse shoved two needles into each hip and I was drugged. I have had to be in some kind of psychiatric care ever since."

I was abhorred and speechless. She was getting restless now and asked me if it would be all right to dust the items in the clothing section.

"I like to keep moving around," she explained.

I certainly did not need any explanation and told her to do whatever felt good to her in the moment. I knew instinctively that she would tell me more of her story at some later time. I watched her take great pride in her dusting and cleaning; she was very efficient at it. I mused that it was just another way for her to survive and stay above the deep psychic pain that she carried. Like other people who lost their awareness in adulthood, she had done so out of extreme pain. It had built up in layers, she had no outlet; her consciousness was crushed. I could identify with her. Fighting the dust balls seemed easier than asserting myself and demanding accountability in terms of addressing abuse as I experienced it. So often we are encouraged as good girls and women to get caught in understanding others' intentions and missing our reality. Over time, we end up missing our pain because it was missed at important developmental stages of our lives. We become adept at normalizing the abnormal and finding fault with the self.

Two men entered the store just minutes later and told us that they had come from Vancouver to explore White Rock. They added that it was a long time since they had been in the area but that they had remembered Daisy's store when it was located on Marine Drive. I told them to take their time browsing and they moved to the clothing section where Betty was dusting. She automatically struck up a conversation with them and seemed very comfortable. She told them that this was a new job for her and that she was taking it very seriously.

My friend, Adriana, came into the store and headed for the clothing section after we greeted one another. She had been to Daisy's many times before. Soon I could hear raucous laughter coming from the room. My friend has an infectious laugh. When I walked in to see what was taking place I saw one of the men modeling a straw hat. He wanted the two women present to comment on how it looked and then he tried several others just for fun. They all seemed to be having a good time. When the men came to the counter, Betty engaged them in a conversation about England. She went on to tell them that she had lived in both England and California.

"I was the most popular girl in the school when I lived in California."

The men humored her and asked her further questions about people she had known and places she might have been to. The situation bordered on pathos for me and I was not at all sure what part was truth and what part illusion because she presented her story so earnestly. There was a light humored dynamic taking place and I did not say much. Adriana had come to the counter in the middle of the conversation where she stood watching silently.

The three of them were ready to leave and Betty said to the men, "Please come back again because I like you."

I felt sad as I witnessed this woman so innocently trying to connect with these passers-by. They were good enough to say, "We like you too, and we will be back."

The men left and she turned to my friend saying, "I love you." and Betty leaned to kiss her.

Adriana was very compassionate and she replied, "I love you too, and I will see you again." They hugged one another.

I felt both sadness and tenderness in my heart for the rest of the day. I have been a therapist for many years and there isn't much that I have not heard. Some stories cut me deeper than others. The innocence and naiveté that I witnessed in this woman who had suffered so much violent abuse touched me at the core of my being. I felt vicariously traumatized. Here I was volunteering at a thrift shop and writing a book based on my experience at Daisy's store, and I was left to wonder at the mystery that was taking place at this stage of my life. I was beginning to pay closer attention to the times when I was feeling my energy drain from me.

I knew deep in my soul that Daisy had heard many stories in her lifetime. Now, as I observe her in present time, I realize that she has been able to sustain her vision because she chose to meet those who came to her where they were at and not try to fix them. She was most interested in giving them a safe place and a sense of love and belonging. She sets appropriate limits, advises them when she feels it necessary and sends them love and blessings from her heart when she feels frustrated with them. This does not mean that she isn't stern when she feels that it is appropriate.

I have personally experienced the bivalency of this elder integrated woman who can be fierce, as well as generous in a self-assertive manner. I knew that I was being asked unconsciously by Betty to be a high witness for her this day, and I respected my own journey in terms of the art of active listening. I just needed to learn to protect myself more from internalizing so much. Having a childhood history of feeling that I had to manage my mother's and father's internal states in order to feel safe had set me up to internalize too much. I needed to let go of that reflex sooner than I had been before I suffered from energy loss and burn out.

Betty kept mentioning throughout the day that she intended to quit smoking in January. I wondered about that intention because I believed that she had unconsciously found a way to stay above her depression and feel grounded.

She shared with me, "I will have to keep busy and do more cleaning if I stop smoking." She started moving then and wanted to show me how she could dance. "I just love to dance and dance and sometimes I sing when I am dancing." I stood as a witness to her joy and praised her.

"It is wonderful to watch you dance, Betty and don't ever stop singing or dancing." At the psycho-emotional level, smoking often has to do with smoldering passions and emotions.

Betty is not aware that there might be a smorgasbord in life and she settles for rice cakes outside of her awareness. She is being cared for by the system and has become as courageous and creative as she can, in a very difficult life score. She started to speak to me in streams of consciousness, "I will bring lots of men to Daisy's because they like me but there will be no sex." I remained silent. "I will attract lots of people to this store to help Daisy," she added. She walked towards the stairs then intending to dust the kitchen wares. She finished while I was busy with the jewelry. She had a small chrome teapot in her hands when she came down the stairs.

"My mother would love this for Christmas. Can I buy it?"

"Most certainly," I said, "just put it with the broach and you can pay next Wednesday."

Daisy phoned me soon after as she usually does on the day that I operate the store on my own.

Betty had the teapot in her hand and said, "Ask Daisy how much this is."

I did just that and Daisy responded, "For Betty it is $2.00."

I assured Daisy that all was well and that my recruit seemed to be enjoying herself. I said nothing about any of her disclosures. Betty discovered the Windex wipes and was meticulously shining her treasure. I felt such tenderness in my heart watching her take so much delight in this gift intended for her mother.

"This is so beautiful, Sandra. My mom will just love it." She beamed with sheer delight.

I wondered how a mother might feel when a daughter like Betty, a radiant, vivacious girl, had lost her mind. Some of these daughters hung themselves in their hospital rooms. Betty wanted to give her mother treasures. It all seems so simple yet so complex. I had to wonder about the level of consciousness that I so bravely sought as I prepared to close the store for the day. I had observed Betty making her mother matter to her and she so wanted to show her love for her through these gifts. She was certainly quite aware of her mother's tastes and needs. She did not leave herself out of the equation though. She chose a sweater that she liked to add to her pile of treasures. I asked her whether she wanted to try it on before she left and she assured me that she felt it was a perfect fit.

I tallied up the price of the treasures and the total came to $15.00.

"I will bring the money next week when I come. I want to pay Daisy $20.00 though, because I want to be fair to her and let her know how grateful I am to have this time with you." She looked straight into my eyes as she spoke.

I was touched and felt as though I had just received some kind of blessing. This woman contains a beautiful spirit and on a deep instinctual level she represents a love that we should all feel for our mothers, the Earth Mother and ourselves. She is an example of the ravaged feminine and the 'unravished' bride. I could not help but think about the many women out there that had experienced variations on the same theme because of a 'robber bridegroom' in their psyches or in the topside world. I believe that the sickest people out there possess high intuition for others' vulnerabilities. In warring cultures, where rape and pillaging are still extant, the tears that women cry have not seemed to matter.

I need to rest and feel as though I am going to cry. Perhaps I need that warm wash right now. It all seems too much. I was feeling overwhelmed! I had probably taken on too much at many levels.

21

"I believe that true identity is found in creative activity springing from within. It is found paradoxically when one loses oneself. Women can best re-find themselves by losing themselves in some kind of creative activity of their own."

Anne Morrow Lindbergh

I have had to put my pen down for a few days because I have been into sorting both on the material plane as well as the psychic plane. I am recalling a Russian folktale in this moment called 'The Vasalisa'.

A young woman who was motherless found her way to the hut of the Baba Yaga who, (according to the story), happened to be the most frightening woman alive. Her stepmother and stepsisters were jealous of Vasalisa and wanted to get rid of her. They told her that she had to go on this difficult quest to find the old woman in order to bring them back some fire because there was no heat in their cabin. This was their ruse to get the old Baba Yaga to kill her and eat her.

When Vasalisa reached the hut of the formidable woman, the girl was required to perform certain tasks. These were requisites that had to do with learning to tolerate the Baba Yaga with all of her fierceness. This was an initiation for her in terms of understanding the tasks of feminine development.

The old woman directed the girl to sweep the yard and then the house as her first task. Then she had to prepare food and separate the mildewed corn from the good corn and to see that everything was in good order. Vasalisa learned that these tasks were ones that an initiate would come back to over and over again as she moved to a different level of consciousness and further healing of her injured feminine instincts. Vasalisa was very naïve in the world and she could be taken advantage of in terms of her good nature. Her mother had taught her to touch a doll in her pocket that would remind her to develop her instincts, and this task was what she was going to learn more about from the Baba Yaga.

I found myself sorting things for Daisy in order to make it easier for her to enjoy what she has created over many years. She was not asking me to do this. I was also doing it to facilitate getting items moving so that she could meet her rental obligations. It was reflexive for me to make it my responsibility by assuming her needs, and I had an unconscious longing to be appreciated. When customers came in, they would often comment that they were overwhelmed with so much stuff, and so I sorted, threw out and cleaned. I became aware experientially how sorting made sense in the interior world as well as the exterior world. A psychic cleansing was going on inside of me at an unconscious level, but I had been working on strengthening my wounded feminine instincts for a very long time.

I was feeling that I had been back in a place in time that I thought that I had already left and healed. There was something coming back to haunt me in my personal life, and I did not trust my instincts about the dilemma I was in. I just knew that the psychic distress that I was feeling meant that something had been healed, and I could not tolerate as much as I used to. In other words, I was not in a place of wanting to understand in order to tolerate oppression, and usury.

The question arose for me, did I have to recognize once again that I had been taken advantage of in terms of my vulnerabilities and sensibilities? Was I giving my power away again? Every once in a while I would get into a dilemma and a few months would pass before I realized that I was doing it again. When I realized it, I was extremely frightened because it happens like a thief coming in the night. Someone comes and steals your power away and you don't even know it for a moment. Many women will give up their power if they are afraid of the unknown, the future.

I was without a support system in White Rock when I made some questionable decisions as I look back in this moment of my writing. I was a co-relater in terms of a conspiracy of silence as well. I was just beginning to notice that and I felt isolated from others because of the lies I was telling myself. I had to open up to Daisy and tell her the truth of my experience. I was in the hut of the Baba Yaga and she had some conscious fire to give me!

"My mother used to tell us that we needed to go outside and eat some dirt and get some grit," Daisy had pointed this out to me several times wagging her index finger in the air. She obviously saw the blueberry-eyed maiden in me who needed a lesson.

Ernie got his pressure cooker yesterday and he was excited about cooking his pork hocks and sauerkraut. We did not receive any suspenders or shirts with snap buttons yet in the donation bags, but Daisy and I have assured him that eventually his needs would be met.

Rick comes in and goes out several times a day. He brings coffee and hot chocolate for Daisy and me. He seems to enjoy the camaraderie and Daisy treats him like a son. He reveres her as if she was his mother. There is much laughter shared by the three of us most days as we try to get creative in terms of the store. It is close to Christmas and we have been doing a lot of decorating with things that Daisy has collected over the years.

Winnie, who already had a broken arm, fell in the driveway yesterday when Patty came to drive Daisy and her home. She tripped over the curb and of course was without balance because of her broken arm. She tried to break her fall with the other hand and fractured her other wrist. Daisy and Patty had to take her to the emergency room at the hospital where she was examined and then admitted. Daisy informed me when I went in to help today that Winnie was admitted for several days, because it was also discovered that she was very anemic and that problem might have contributed to the number of falls that she has suffered lately.

Stacey was in the store with Winnie yesterday, as well, because it was her day to work. I was amazed when I asked her about her accent that she began to smile and open up to me. I guessed that that was why she often sat and just watched me. I think now that it was all about trust. I learned that she was from Cape Town, South Africa, and that she and her family had come to North America by boat when she was thirteen years old. They landed in New York before moving to Toronto and then to Sarnia, Ontario where they lived for several years. When I shared with her that I had a practice in Sarnia for seven years she told me that her father worked for an oil company there. She proudly stated, "I went from grade nine to thirteen at two high schools in the city before I attended Humber College, in Toronto, where I studied fashion design."

I had a sense that Stacey had been arrested in her development when she was in her early twenties. I have already hypothesized earlier in the book that perhaps she experienced little opportunity to be heard into speech. Her accent is different and she has a shy demeanor. I have a sense that she has the capacity to truly see, and I am certain that she was, and is, highly sensitive. I took the risk of asking her about her depression that was evident to me. She shared, "It began soon after I graduated from college." I had the feeling from the first time that I met Stacey that she was much brighter than she appeared to let on. I told her that I knew about depression from first hand experience and that we had some commonality in that area.

I offered her some insight, "It is my personal belief depression is the opiate of oppression which dulls our senses and keeps us from becoming aware and seeking the truth of our existence."

She smiled at me knowingly as she nodded her head and whispered, "I agree, Sandra."

"Have you ever experienced talk therapy, Stacey?" I was attempting to get her to speak her truth.

"No, I have just been given drugs by psychiatrists." We did not have any more talk time, so I was left to ponder what might have happened to traumatize this girl-woman in her blossoming. Was she another woman who was interrupted through some kind of abuse in her individuation process, which means becoming self-aware?

Stacey, at forty-two years of age, continues to live with her parents. I was the same age when I went to graduate school and attempted to complete my own task of individuation. This task had been complicated by my mother's addiction to alcohol and my propensity to become more other directed than inner directed. In psychological terms, it is a concern about one having an external locus of control over an internal locus of control. I was deeply ensconced in the role of caretaker. I have spent years trying to understand the difference between taking care, which was a reflexive defense masking my own pain, and choosing to give care. My focus had been to try to fix my mother so that I would be able to bond enough in order to take leave of her and grow up still feeling emotionally and spiritually connected. I was making a conscious choice in the moment concerning my connection with Stacey at this point in time.

I was also aware that too much light, too soon, is not good and I ended the conversation. I felt that I had helped her by being fully present. My hope for her is that someone will see her light in this lifetime and lift her up. To be honest, that is probably a projection on my part because that was my greatest need.

Vasalisa received just enough light from the Baba Yaga to burn through to the truth of the lies that had been told to her. She was able to carry the fire of consciousness even though it meant a great deal of responsibility for her. There were many times that she wanted to throw the fire away out of fear, and it took great courage for her to carry the light of consciousness. I was just another pilgrim who was a few steps up the road from someone like Stacey, and I decided to take her hand gently for the short time that I would be in her presence.

Luva Lynne was leaving for Guatemala to pick up new items to sell and she came in to see Daisy while Vicki was there. It was another Friday and Vicki's day to dust. Luva Lynne witnessed Vicki's behavior for the first time. Daisy mentioned to Luva Lynne in front of me, "It might be a good idea to lay her off for two Fridays with pay."

I have shared my opinion with the reader earlier in the book and with Daisy that I felt that Vicki should be in another facility other than the one that she was in, for her own sake as well as for the sake of others who had to be exposed to her behavior every day. She has an incredible capacity to incite rage. It is difficult for the best therapists to deal with that dynamic, let alone those around her who are already unstable. She also has no impulse control as a result of the brain damage. This dynamic puts Daisy in a difficult position. It is one thing to feel compassion because of the nature of her injuries, and another to feel it for oneself so that one does not become victimized. I believe that we must not tolerate what one experiences as abuse, regardless of the intention of the perpetrator.

If I sound frustrated, I am!

I was also becoming acutely aware that Daisy was losing her patience with some of her charges. Perhaps this is a good thing, in terms of being able to become more reflective about what she has already contributed in her life, and where she might want to invest her life energy now. It is for me, as well, to contemplate, and we are both at the Crossroads. I have come to know and understand more as I move into the later years of my life about how important it is to honor the death bringing aspect of the Crone energy.

I have come to realize the importance of bringing appropriate endings to ways of being, in order to support the new life that wants to live within me. I have lived in a fear based culture, as we all have, but there was always an aspect in me that would not let me settle for too long in places with people and ways of being that were not life enhancing. I walked in a somnambulistic state at times because denial was a way to maintain my shaky self. I could not anaesthetize the pain of deadness and capture with chemicals. I had to keep facing the pain of becoming more fully alive over and over again. I have come to understand my mother's life mainly so that I can get on with my own. She couldn't set me free, which is every daughter's wish, but the task was for me to free myself. It is difficult in this politic, but times are changing. I believe that younger women have to come to know the difficulties of those women who came before them and the courage that it has taken for many of them to create the inroads for them.

There exists an instinct in all of us that demands that we embrace that part of us that is comfortable with death and the concept of: 'what is enough'? The body is the feminine ground in men and women, and when it begins to act out, we have gone too far in terms of abusing it. We do the same to the Earth Mother, and as a culture, we are so unconscious of 'what is enough'. This is the 'life-death-life' knowing in women. Women not so wounded in their natural feminine instincts and those who have healed carry this deep knowing. They do not fear death because they have learned to make friends with their death aspect, and have become more than comfortable with bringing appropriate endings.

This comfort with bringing death is natural to our blood cycles as well. The uterus sloughs off at the end of every month to prepare for new life. The older woman holds the blood and carries wisdom when the Mother time is over. 'What is enough' helps us to become comfortable with decisions that might seem cruel to others, especially if our behaviors have been about compliancy and expected reliability that enforced over-identification with Mother Energy.

We cannot maintain our Maiden energy or vital life without the fierceness and grounding of the Crone aspect within. The mandate of subordination has been bred into women through the concept of exaggerated reverence for the Holy Mother archetype and the fear of elder women. As far as I have experienced personally, as well as in my practice as a feminist therapist, this idea leads us to become dry boned and wizened, well before the body knows how to age. The too good Mother in us has to die so that we can maintain our intrinsic creative and vital natures.

22

"With support, we find a way for the wounds of our individual histories to be a collective doorway to living our purpose."

Dawna Markova

When I met Daisy in the store today an old friend of the very same age of ninety- one years came to see Daisy with a few bags in her arms. I started to put away the donations while they spoke. The woman kept showing a vest to Daisy that her sister had knitted. I was amused after what I had written yesterday when I witnessed Daisy in her fierceness even with an old friend. She told her friend in no uncertain terms that the vest was outdated and the wool in it was not good. She stated, "I could not sell that here especially at your asking price of $40.00. If you want to donate it that is fine, but it does not even belong in the store."

Her old friend left with the vest, and Daisy turned to me as she often does with a comment that made me laugh. "She needs to come to the party and know what's going on. She lives in Florida part time too, and brings back shells for me to sell and she can see that I have too many already."

I notice Daisy's humor more and more. I think it is because she knows that she can say things to me and I get it. I am also becoming more aware of my need to be with the like-minded because there is such an ease that comes with peer knowing or, might I say feeling a sense of real belonging with one's pack!

I have not seen Betty since she worked with me on that

Wednesday when she disclosed some of her story to me. Her worker confirmed to me that her stories were true. She has been heavily medicated in the last while. When she called me at the store today, I could not make sense of anything she said. This was in such contrast to her behavior the day when she worked with me and seemed to have had such a good time. I am not sure that I will see her again in the store, and I feel sad.

I sat with Daisy for a break and told her about the conversation with Betty, and she just shook her head. She asked me whether I would like to mentor two new recruits. Speaking my truth at this point in time, I am happiest when some of them are not there to work. I wonder if Daisy has reached that point too, and if she has, why she might keep hanging on to that original vision she had for them?

"I will need some time to think about that, Daisy," I commented.

Jane comes every Tuesday to put her time in for the government allowance. She immediately finds a chair and just sits there looking depressed until Daisy instructs her to do something. She does as little as possible, sighing the whole time, and then heads for the chair again. She speaks only when spoken to and uses one or two syllable words. I believe that she gets something out of playing dumb, but then it might be my low level of toleration at this point in time. I find her most frustrating. I also have observed that when the customers come in, her energy affects them because they do not stay in the store for long.

Trying to change the subject, I asked Daisy about her brother Archie, who was diagnosed as challenged mentally. She said, "He was what most in those days would call a slow learner. He was very good natured and everybody loved and enjoyed him." She smiled as she shared this story:

"One Christmas, when Archie was in his sixties, he wanted a Santa Claus suit. His habit was to go daily for early coffee at Twelfth Avenue and Broadway in Vancouver. He rode the bus every day. We got him the suit and he wore it to the coffee shop where he said, 'Ho! Ho! Ho!' He shook everybody's hands wishing them a very 'Merry Christmas'. When he was walking down the street to catch the bus two children saw him and yelled, "There is Santa!" The family asked him in for hot chocolate and it made his Christmas."

I asked Daisy to refresh my mind in terms of where he was in the sibling line.

"He was second from the last born into the family and he went to Woodland School in New Westminster as a child, and so I was not too aware of the struggle. Archie lived with Mother until she could no longer keep him, and he came to live at my house."

When I asked her about her experience with him she began; "One night in Vancouver, a street lady that pushed a cart was found in a dumpster after someone had murdered her. Two weeks later Archie did not show up at his usual time. I called the police because Archie had coffee with them every morning and they liked him so much that they had given him a police hat and jacket. I asked if they would search the dumpster because I was extremely worried. The police told me to call them back if he did not show up before eleven o'clock. At five minutes to eleven Archie walked in to say he had been at a wrestling match watching Kiniski and that he took the bus home. What could I say - I was just so relieved that he was safe, but it gave me quite a scare."

I learned that Archie lived with Daisy for several years but she could not determine the exact amount of time. She told me, "I taught him basic skills so he would be able to care for himself, and these included grooming, how to make sandwiches and how to handle money." With pride she commented, "He was able to travel to Hawaii by himself."

She continued, "While Archie was with me, I took in this girl who was having drug and alcohol problems and was trying to rehabilitate. I got her a job in another thrift store and she got well. Archie took quite a liking to her and she took a liking to him mostly on a friendship level, although I knew that Archie would have liked the relationship to be much more than that.

She decided to go to Kamloops, to work and she invited Archie to go with her. She was very good to him, and then he took sick and died of liver cancer."

I sat listening to Daisy and watching her expressions, and all I can share with you in this moment is that I am amazed at the tenacity and strength of this woman who continued to be strong in the face of difficult situations. I identify with her so much in that I know now that my strength has sometimes been my weakness at times. I am very uncomfortable with reaching out for help when I need it. I guess that I saw that as a weakness or perhaps I possessed an intrinsic sense of unworthiness. I believe that I was set up early to meet others' high expectations that I always seemed to carry them off, until it almost killed me. I work constantly on trying to be gentle with myself and to accept humility as a very human condition. I feel that I am being humbled now, and that I am getting down low as I accept my human limitations.

I will not stop to perfect this work. I will get it down and that is important to me and the woman, Daisy Walls, whom I have come to know, love and respect.

23

> "To find someone's spot of grace, ask him or her about their favorite scar made of the strongest tissue even though they result in great injury."
>
> *Clarissa Pinkola Estes*

It was a dark December day and customers were few. I had more time with Daisy than I normally have. We were able to continue the conversation from the day before. Daisy spoke today of her son, Barry who, like her brother Archie, was diagnosed as 'challenged'. Daisy admitted that it was very difficult for her husband and her to accept it and after travelling to specialists even in the United States, they came to grips with the truth.

She shared, "Eventually, our whole family went for testing and we found out that my mother carried the gene for retardation."

I felt a deep sadness as Daisy went on. "Barry eventually married a girl who was also challenged and had emotional problems. Barry was not one to confide in me and so I had to learn to let him be. I found out that her father had sexually assaulted his wife and that her mother covered her with ugly clothes that matched the shame. She would wake up in the night afraid. Over time, Barry took sick with boils all over his legs. Doctors were not able to diagnose the problem. His wife could not handle him when he got sick. He would be seventy this year. He died four years ago."

I have always had a sad but tender heart, and my heart hurt as I listened to Daisy these past two days. I began to understand her need to create a program to help the mentally challenged, and how she was able to tolerate much more than most could in terms of their special needs. Perhaps she was a woman who decided to free her own nature and longed for a culture to go with it. This yearning can make a person go on, in spite of difficult times. If Daisy could not find a culture that encouraged her, then she decided to construct it herself. I wonder if she really knows how special she is, at so many levels. I pray that this writing becomes a testimonial and as tribute to her strength of spirit in difficult times. The roots of my spirit grew deep in this work.

Daisy went on to tell me about being with her mother on her deathbed. She shared, "I talked to my mother before she died and tried to make sure that she understood that she did nothing wrong in terms of having a child who was challenged. There was so much shame associated with it at the time."

I certainly understood because I worked for four summers at The Ontario Children's Hospital when I attended university. I had had first hand experience with the shame, blame and guilt that so many families suffered as a result of having a 'special needs' child born into the family.

I stood at my mother's death bed two years ago and used witch hazel to soothe her because it was available on her night table. She had been on heavy doses of morphine for pain that caused her skin to itch. I felt as though I was anointing her and a deeper understanding occurred between us. I used a cotton pad to soothe her eyes, and I stroked her cheeks and hair. All that she could speak as she passed in my arms was, "Sandra, Sandra, Sandra." In those moments of higher consciousness I felt that it was her way of validating her different child. She passed away in peace. I knew that my spirit had chosen her to be my Earth mother and it would be through her that I would come to deeper consciousness of my innate spirituality. She enabled me to be able to relate to Daisy over time. The student was ready and the teacher appeared. I had come to understand that my mother was a talented, creative, and beautiful woman who did not have the support she needed and she drank herself to death.

24

> "Let it be known that we need many mothers in this lifetime…so long are we from Avalon when the moon tides did run in our blood."
>
> Sandra C. Johnston

Daisy and I had more time together between customers and she spoke more with me about her mother. "I had very little time with my mother; it seemed that she could only deal with one of us at a time. There always seemed to be a competition amongst my sisters and me for Mother's love. I also have recognized that my mother had a difficult time showing love."

I was resonating with her at a very deep level as I recognized that we had that experience in common as well. I have spent a great deal of time trying to understand my mother and her behavior towards me and how different she was with my sisters. I believe that she split off that part of herself that she could not embrace, and I contained her projections of her despised self. I was treated most harshly and she imposed very high expectations upon me.

Through experience with many women in my practice, I have come to know that it is very difficult for mothers in our culture and it has been so for a very long time. There has not been a feminine face of God for centuries and we live in a mother blaming culture. Even though a woman's culture may have seemed to evolve into more conscious reasoning, the internal mother within us will have the same ideas about what a mother should look like and act like as those in the culture of our childhood. In Jungian psychology, this is called the Mother Complex and it becomes a core aspect of a woman's psyche. We must be able to recognize its condition, strengthen certain aspects, understand those that serve us, dismantle those aspects that stifle us, and begin over again if necessary.

There is an ambivalent mother, a collapsed mother and an 'unmothered' mother. We would be able to help ourselves, if we could understand these mothering structures. A complex that exists within each of our psyches might need adjustment if we realize that some energy within does not sustain those qualities that we can determine are unique to us.

The ambivalent mother is one that is made aware through the comments of others that her child is different from the so-called norm. She cannot take a stand for herself and her child and what she believes in. Many women in our historical past have been murdered physically, psychically, and spiritually for protecting her child or another woman's child who was seen as different. Most women feel this threat deep in their unconscious and move to groom that child in terms of the culture's expectations, regardless of the child's deep needs. This child is at great risk of losing her/his true self. Often, this mother is 'unmothered' herself and the child within herself has been persecuted. Ambivalence means the state of being pulled in many directions. This mother feels torn between loving her child and being accepted by her community.

A collapsed mother can no longer endure the torment she receives from her community as she attempts to protect that 'different' child. When a mother collapses, she has lost her sense of herself. When a woman has a collapsed mother complex in her psyche, she will be wobbly about her worth. She might even feel that choices between fulfilling outer demands and the demands of the soul are life and death matters. She will go around feeling tormented like an outsider who belongs nowhere. What is not normal is to sit and moan about it but rather, do something about it and go off in search of what one belongs to. This is always the next step for anyone who feels exiled or has an internal collapsed mother. She must stand up and refuse to become one herself!

The most common kind of fragile mother is the 'unmothered' mother. She is so often more intent on having babies that she essentially turns away from the child or children she has. Often she is an 'unmothered' woman herself and holds naive presentiments about herself and others. She is very psychically dislocated and often feels unlovable even by her babies. A mother must be consciously mothered in terms of mothering her own offspring. She does not suddenly become a temporal mother all by herself. In earlier times, there were women who were always there to nurture the young mothers through hands or words.

First time mothers, especially, need an older woman to teach her Crone wisdom. Every new mother begins as a child mother and she needs the direction of older woman, no matter how old she might be. This is the female-to-female nutritional system that we have been missing for far too long. These older women held the blood and the instinctual knowing and behaviors. They could teach and invest the younger mother with the same. This knowing was not just given through words but also through a look, a touch with the palm of the hand, a murmur or a special kind of hug.

My hands were crippling and I had to come to realize that they were beings in their own right. My body was talking and having the last word and it was going to help me to see where I was blind.

Daisy took my hurting hands into hers and rubbed them with her medicine. "You will be cured of this," she ministered.

My hands were hurting; I was bound away from being able to comfort myself. I could not self heal and as much as I had helped others to heal, I was still following an age-old path of self sacrifice. I could do nothing now but grieve. I could see, touch and feel the feminine face of God in Daisy and I would grow to love her in myself. Daisy took time today to teach me some important truths about life and relationships. When we were about to shut everything down for the day, she moved to embrace me with a long hug and the words, "I care a great deal about you."

I, in turn, whispered into her ear, "You are my spiritual mother who is making sure that I come into full blossom, and I thank you for it." I have had this level of honest support and encouragement from my other two spiritual mothers with over eighty years of wisdom, Jessie O'Neill and Anne Griffith from Chatham, Ontario before my travels to British Columbia. They were there for me in ways that my mother could not be. Daisy, Jessie and Anne had the heroism and the strength to stand for what they saw and I have come to know swan mothers and recognize my people. I am not saying that ducks are bad, but I am not an ugly duckling.

Belonging is a blessing and I am truly blessed. It does not matter that I am in my sixties; a child mother can be any age, and Daisy is teaching me to learn to mother myself and to recognize my true worth.

25

> "I have no idea whence this tide comes, or where
> it goes, but when it begins to rise in my heart,
> I know that a story is in the offing."
> *Dorothy Canfield*

Daisy invited me to sit beside her as soon as I arrived into the store. She wanted me to know how Winnie was doing post surgery,

"The doctors found another tumor in her abdomen when they operated. The cancer was in the bowel and they think that they got it."

"That is good, Daisy. It certainly is a mystery how all of this was discovered after her fall in front of the store," I commented.

"Yes, they found the anemia and then the cancer."

"There are no accidents, when one sees it in this way."

"You know, Sandra, how she is with the animals alive or stuffed? She is supposed to let her left arm be straight so that it will heal faster but she has this stuffed lamb that she cuddles with that arm and will not stop."

Earlier in the book, I shared with you that Winnie has a propensity to talk to the stuffed animals in the store. Rick brought a stuffed Santa that he wished to donate into the store that day that she fell and it became 'alive' for her right away. I told Rick that he might consider taking it to the hospital when he went to visit her next. He thought it was a good idea; he had witnessed her conversation with Santa. Daisy and I continued to share some about the importance of being able to support each person's uniqueness and of how different the world might become if we were, all of us, to become more conscious of that.

While we were engaged in discourse about this issue, Will, who was a mental health worker, came into the store with two young women who were in his charge. One of them he introduced as Agnes who had been making jewelry in the store when I first met Daisy. She had offered to make me a pair of earrings to match a necklace that I was interested in but was concerned about finding earrings to go with it. She was very creative and I was very pleased with what she made. She was in the store this particular day to pick up some things that she had left with Daisy after taking her leave from the store.

Will introduced the other young woman as Molly.

"That is such a beautiful name, Molly," I commented.

She had the face of a picture of a beautiful Irish girl. I mentioned the jewelry that we had on the sale table to her. By looking at her, I could not help but wonder why she was in Will's care. I watched as she began to have a conversation with the jewelry as the other customers were entering. I became aware of the schizophrenia then. When the others entered, she decided to exit and stood just outside of the store door like an outsider seemingly happy to carry on a conversation with the fire hydrant. I was curious about that rich inner life that she had inside of her and why she had to leave the topside world in order to tap into it.

I wanted to ask, "Who has hurt you, my dear?"

Daisy had commented to me earlier in the day about Winnie and her affinity for animals animate or inanimate. "She understands something that others don't," Daisy had commented. Molly also was completely immersed in a world that no one else could understand.

I have come to the awareness myself, that it should not matter who understands as long as I do in terms of behavior that I might choose for myself if it is working. One might name this process a 'recovery from an addiction to outside approval or external locus of control'. Yet, this 'other-directedness' has been a part of the socialization process for women since the beginning of patriarchy. It is one of the elements of capture of a woman's soul life. It is like saying, "Take that talented one (we are all born gifted) and socialize her in the extreme in terms of the mandates of the politic."

It is often women who enter their later years who begin to let themselves off this hook if they are lucky. They come to realize that this ruse of being nice becomes a kind of wheedling that has kept them in their subordinate place. They look outside of themselves for the answers particularly from men and women in power positions. Perhaps schizophrenics are just noisier than the rest of us in their depression and do not have to be as accountable as those who choose to go against the grain. Often these wildish women are seen as dissidents or renegades, according to a pathological script.

We have been taught by every institution to follow toxic scripts from a very early age and time of great vulnerability. Those who professed to love us and to have our best interests at heart imposed thoughtless acceptance.

The other elements of capture I mention now are many: overly feminize her in the extreme; never let her know that she is special; wound her in the feminine body so that she will be cut off from her instincts and intuition (thus the rape and incest, that has been extant for centuries); isolate her from others who might comment on her pain; make sure that she associates primarily with those people who are at a lesser level of development; put her next to addictive excesses that help her to be anaesthetized to her suffering whether it be, drugs, alcohol, sex, food, relationships, or power and she will be captured. She will have been set up to live her life in a somnambulistic state of denial. Reverse the process, though, and she will be freed.

I hope this makes you angry! Women's addictions often have to do with unresolved grief over the loss of the true self or the vital girl.

When I chose to write this book, I had no idea how it would flow. Now as I am finding and winding my way through it, I recognize that this has been a way to weave feminist theory through the weaving *of a true story about a woman's life and revelations concerning the connections with the people who came into her life. It is also my story.*

Another woman entered the store that afternoon and introduced herself as Tina and told us that she was Dillon's mother. At first, Daisy and I did not put it together that she was referring to 'Bill' who loved watches. It was my instinct to ask Tina. We broke out laughing when we realized that Daisy and I had been calling Dillon "Bill" all this time! Tina spoke to us of Dillon's respect and love for Daisy, and how he loved to come into the store to see her. Tina wanted to buy the old dresser in the clothing room for Dillon for Christmas. "He has had his eyes on that for a long time," she explained. "It is going to be a surprise for him because he is an antique lover."

Daisy was delighted that Dillon would have the dresser because, "he holds a special place in my heart."

She instructed me to empty it of the underwear, socks, ribbons, lace, and other miscellaneous items. I put them in a Rubbermaid container and helped Tina to load the furniture piece into her car. She appeared to be a very proud mother after she heard Daisy speak so highly of her son. We also shared with her how Dillon found his hat for Halloween in the store, how he would come in often to appraise watches for Daisy, and how we enjoyed his presence.

Vicki had been in the store during this time as well and had mentioned to Tina several times that she always dusted the tops of the clothing racks. She was acting very deferent in front of the customers this particular day after Daisy had castigated her the week before for interrupting her when she was conversing with a customer. I must say that I was surprised by her behavior because it was not her usual way of interacting.

Vicki had entered the store earlier bearing pop cans in several bags. Daisy had an agreement with her that she would make three cents on each can and the other two would go to support a hockey team. She can hardly wait once she receives payment to buy more clothes and her tendency to harp at Daisy begins. It is very sad and difficult to bear at times. Her workers came to give Vicki a ride to the Lodge this particular day. They had introduced themselves as students in the Practical Nursing Program at a local college. They both smiled at me as Vicki kept up her antics and quietly whispered to me that they were happy that this was the last day of their internship at the group home.

Sheila came in with her dog, Star. They came to the store often for a visit. She happened to find a lovely red turtleneck sweater to wear at Christmas and went home to get the cash for it. She brought back two Christmas sweaters of her own to show Daisy. Delaine happened to come in at the same time and began her search for treasures. She came in often to chat with Daisy and me. She was interested in buying the two books that I had already written and said to Daisy, "I can't wait to read them because I enjoy my conversations with Sandra." I felt appreciated and proud.

I was feeling more authentic as the days passed and I met more of Daisy's customers. I had to interact with them, as well as with those who came to work with her. It was much different than sitting across from one client, one at a time that had nothing to do with socializing. I was enjoying the change. I found it very easy to converse with the women who come into the Treasure Trove especially with those who had been examining their lives over time.

To me, this was evidence of women's need to have a nutritional system of females who show care and compassion. They need to have a place to be heard into speech. Some days, I had the sense that Daisy and I were doing subversive work under the umbrella of Modern Services for the Handicapped.

We are, all of us, the walking wounded. No one leaves his or her child hood unscathed and we are challenged by it. Scars can become very real handicaps, especially in relationships, if we do not heal the wounds. Home is the place where our story begins, but we do not have to be our story. My scars were being activated in present time and I needed to do some sorting in order to let go of the migraine of my past. Like Vasalisa, I was moving painfully towards higher consciousness that would help me to burn through to the truth and expose the lies that I had been telling myself. Do not get me wrong, there were many days and times that I would have liked to shut down my awareness like the frightened girl in the Baba Yaga folk tale. I was becoming a wiser woman and I was in the process of leaving the dutiful daughter mentality behind. I would also have to leave people behind who thought that they had my best interests at heart and who had taken advantage of my vulnerabilities.

26

> "The denial of one's feelings can be psychologically and physically exhausting."
>
> *Sandra C. Johnston*

Daisy invited me to sit next to her as soon as I entered the store. She looked sad and she shared with me that she wanted to speak to me about her Native friend, Nick.

"I have learned that he passed away today. He was a brave man who overcame his addiction to alcohol and became a well-known mask carver. Nick was known and loved by many people in the White Rock area."

"I remember seeing him sitting by the pier carving when I took walks in the summer."

"Well, he happened to become a very good friend of mine over time. I sold many of his beautiful masks for him out of my store. Right now I can't even think about him without wanting to cry."

"It sounds like you had a very special bond with Nick, Daisy," I commented. She relaxed into the flow of her tears and spoke to me between sobs.

"He came to me about ten days ago and told me that he was going home to visit with his daughters and his four grandchildren and that he had come to say, "Good-bye" to me. I did not know what he meant. He told me then that he had always loved me."

Daisy was sobbing and I moved to touch her gently on her

arm, not wanting to interrupt her tears. She was letting me see into her depths. "These last few years he was made Chief of his reserve. One of his daughters is presently pregnant with a boy child who will be the next Chief, although he is not born yet. This man became such an example to his people in terms of taking responsibility for his addiction to the 'firewater'. I know now that he had come to say his last farewell to me. He told me that he would make masks until he put his canoe in the water to make his last part of the journey."

I was witnessing a very deep knowing in Daisy. She had admiration for the aboriginal people just as I had and still do. They are clan-making, weaving, planting, sewing engendering people and no matter how difficult life becomes their ways support the soul and psyche. We have much to learn from those who honor the old ways. I am not speaking here about sentimentality or illogical fantasy. Many of these ancient ways are a form of nutrition that never spoils, and actually increases the more one uses them. It is peaceful for the soul to take from past knowledge, present power, and future ideas all at once.

Within minutes of her disclosure to me, a young man and his father came in to wish Daisy a 'Merry Christmas' and to gift her.

Daisy introduced them to me. "Sandra, this is Kevin and Mark who is Kevin's father. Kevin has worked for me doing community service for misdemeanors." Kevin continued to smile while she went on, "Look at what a fine mature man he has become." The two men spent some quality time with her as I busied myself with sorting the donations that had arrived.

After they left, Daisy explained to me that Kevin's mother had died and that he struggled with a great deal of physical pain as a result. "He kept his grief to himself and he was the kind of young man who would never let on that he was hurting. I knew that his pain and anxiety went into his body."

I believed that Daisy wanted me to appreciate his courage as well as his survival defenses. It was so synchronistic that Kevin came in to see Daisy just after she allowed her own tears to flow. She was also creating an opening for the light of my own awareness.

Luva Lynne was back from Guatemala and came in to reconnect with Daisy. I enjoyed her presence and camaraderie whenever she came into the store. She worked on her colorful display of all the wonderful items that she sold to help the struggling people of Guatemala. Her wares were all hand made by these people that she cares so much about. I recognized that her relationship with Daisy had been a long term one, and yet we seemed to be able to talk very freely when we were three together. I was reminded of the times I spent with Jessie and Anne in Chatham.

Rick was in and out several times a day. He seemed to be ready to help Daisy and I with whatever we required at the time and he continued to bring us coffee and hot chocolate. It was wonderful to have someone treat us and, of course, he loved to chat during our break time! He has met another lady and he seems to have a lot of energy lately. I believe that he is very smitten with her. He came in this day and asked me to come around to his lodging because he had a surprise for me. I thought he was going to introduce me to his lady friend.

"I have someone I want you to meet," he said as we headed to his bachelor pad. He opened the door and there sat a beautiful black Labrador retriever who did not even move as I entered."

"This is Annie, Sandra. I named her after Orphan Annie because she is a stray. I am going to take care of her until I find the owner or someone who would like a dog." I stroked orphaned Annie and eventually went back to the store.

I shared with Daisy that I believed that this dog would become very important to Rick over time in terms of his healing journey. He is still in mourning over the loss of his wife in February of this year and could use some unconditional positive regard. This is the first Christmas that he will spend alone.

Daisy nodded affirmatively, "I believe that he was quite

dependent upon his wife and that he's very frightened of moving forward."

"Yes, Daisy, I agree. I am not sure that he knows yet who and what he might consider serving or, who and what he loves. I hope he will to come to recognize his inner gifts and talents and know more definitively what it is that he values. It is the Knight's question in terms of the search for the Holy Grail. I hope that he will come to the light of understanding over time in this third stage of his life instead of engaging in dependency solutions."

I had witnessed vulnerability in both Daisy and Rick this winter day and I felt my own. I took the time to feel the loneliness and the sadness that came with my move to a different province so far from my kin, my adult children and my friends. This time of year makes the pain even more poignant. I knew that I had to pay attention to this pain and not miss it in terms of my usual focus on everyone else's. The events of the day brought me this awareness.

I found comfort in the fact that I had made a deep connection with Daisy as a friend, mentor and wise mother, and with Rick, upon whom I projected the 'brother' I never had. This was the belonging that I needed to get through a difficult life transition. I knew that we are always in transition, but I have found support and care from friends who for now have understanding and compassion. It is a blessing and one I am grateful for at this Christmas tide, and always.

27

"If you can see magic in a fairy tale, you can face the future."
Danielle Steele

Today is Winter Solstice and the longest night of the year. I am sitting at my desk writing as the midnight hour rings in. I have done some resting and allowing of 'revelations' to come from within. These are very important dynamics of this ritual time.

This is a period of Endarkment…the part of the journey that is like the dark side of the moon…unseen. It is the time of the deepest night…where dreams dance. It is the darkness that is the silence of the universe before time began…before Grandmother Crone took a flame from the pocket of her dark cloak and flung the stars into the night. This is the journey of Endarkment…the time of the seed in the silence under the earth. We wait for the changes of warmth that bring new growth. It is the time of the unborn…floating in the waters off the womb…growing silently…waiting for the change to begin…waiting to move to the light of birth. This is the time at the end of living as the body stills and the breath slows…and the spirit is 'midwifed' through the darkness by the Crone who shows the way. This is the journey of Endarkment, where in the silence and the darkness, we can find the flame within…the flame that is the gift of love and light. This is the journey of Endarkment where we wait unseeing…like the new moon in the dark sky…knowing that this is the time of change…of metamorphosis, of love… of magic…the time of healing.

Soon we will begin a cycle of rebirth…for now…we wait.

Daisy is reciting the melody of her life to me and I not only write the lines but I am learning to read between them. I am healing my instincts and intuition the more time I spend with her, both watching and listening to her.

Sometimes in my everyday world, I resent being disturbed in my reveries and feel much like someone with schizophrenia might. No one will bother them because they are often seen as crazy and impossible. I have the awareness that I am not crazy and I feel anger when my friend, Garth, disturbs my creative flow because he does not understand the inner workings of a creative soul, especially a writer's. I continue to live in a climate where I am not feeling understood in terms of my needs for needing to experience events directly, for staring into space at times, for writing late into the night and thinking thoughts that had to germinate from the soil of my fertile instincts and that passion did not always mean engaging in sex. I felt that sex was overrated especially at this stage of my life. Companionship and a sense of community had become very important to me.

I have had the experience over and over again of being seen as distant and impossible, when all I needed was some time alone to traverse the terrain of my unconscious and eventually bring what I discovered into the topside world. This is demonstrated not only in my writing but also in my thinking, actions and behavior. I bore witness to the amount of support that was in place for the mentally and physically challenged, and I wonder, at this point in my life when I am left to do so much alone, and without support, what it would be like to be held in my exception. I had held my parents and many others throughout my lifetime and I longed for a holding environment where I would be witnessed in my process without advice and attempts to motivate me. I recognized that I experienced little support for what I was trying to do in terms of helping others. I was getting to the point of not being able to help myself.

Daisy spoke to me today, "You know, Sandra, some of us do not understand you because you are a writer, and it is your responsibility to teach what you know."

That has always been a longing of mine and most of my degrees are in education but I have had major issues trying to find people who are willing to map new psychic territory because it would take a great deal of resiliency. The process would mean perceiving and honoring change as the only constant. So many of us have been steeped for centuries in a fear-based culture with a politic bent on maintaining status quo, capitalistic economy and national security in the form of armaments.

Yes, I have somehow found my place at Daisy's, and I am one of the challenged and have been handicapped. Daisy tells me that I have to "get your feet out of the mud" and Rick tells me that "You have to take your boots off." At this point in time, I am not sure what they mean, but good drama keeps me guessing in terms of the outcome. I will stay until the end of my writing time. Like the long distance runner, I know the last lap will be the most difficult and so on I write…I ask you to keep your minds and your hearts open.

It was closing time and I asked Daisy what she wanted me to do with the things that I had removed from the dresser that she sold to Dillon's mother.

She directed me, "Just leave them in a container with a sign on them saying what is there and the customers can rummage through them. Perhaps you and I can make some grab bags over time but not right now." I was relieved because I was getting tired.

I retrieved a precious memory of the happy times that my sisters and I had with my dad in his store. My father often instructed us to make 'grab bags' out of the bigger bags of seasonal candy that was 'not moving' in store talk. It was exciting for the kids who bought them to have to guess what they might find inside the mystery bags. Every one of the "penny candy kids" as my dad would call them, left the store excited with their treasures and I felt joy just watching them. Perhaps this is where my interest in treasure and thrift shops started. I decided that this might be a good thing to do with some of the small children's toys that were just sitting in baskets. I believed that they would move faster. This would be a repeat experience form of creativity and pleasure that I had working in my dad's store.

I have heard the saying that, "before enlightenment, chop wood and carry water; after enlightenment, chop wood and carry water." After all of the achieving I have done in my life perhaps for the wrong reasons, I have found delight once again in something so very simple and ordinary.

I mentioned to Daisy while we were turning out the lights and bringing closure to the day that I had not sent any Christmas cards.

"We can't be expected to do everything," Daisy quipped with her Crone wisdom once again.

It was very sobering and I was remembering my mom making sure that she had done everything possible to personally carry out the Christmas myth before she settled down to drink away or, should I say, bottle her resentment, and take it out on me in unconscious stupor. She was just one of the tarnished angels of the culture who were living the good woman script and hated every minute of having to live up to those imposed expectations. It was bottled rage. It certainly protected everyone from a show of righteous anger, except for me who contained her hostility in my body, mind and spirit. I unconsciously defended against any display of anger and turned it inward toward myself. I became just as depressed as she did in spite of my competence.

Daisy's answer to me was all that I needed to do was to remind me to mother myself and not worry about what others think. You see, I had to do some sorting again at another level of development in the hut of the Baba Yaga! I consciously decided that a note to those I love and miss after Christmas, when I had more time and felt less pressure, would mean more to me and to them in terms of quality and meaning. Besides, we are such a Hallmark culture that we seem to have to rely on occasions and others' words to show we care.

This day, many people who had come to know, value and appreciate Daisy came to gift and greet her for the Christmas season. Once again, I left with a treasure trove of warm feelings.

28

> "One's purpose is merely knowing where one's talents and the needs of the world intersect."
>
> *Aristotle*

Betty showed up at the store today after two weeks absence. A new worker arranged her schedule because Kirsten had given up in terms of making things better for Betty She was frustrated with the amount of medication her charge had been given. I recognized right away that Betty was far more drugged than the last time I saw her. Betty informed Daisy and I right away that she had quit smoking. Daisy wanted me to take her under my wings again today and direct her in terms of assisting me in the store. I simply asked her, "If this was your store, Betty, what do you see right now that needs doing?"

She replied, "I think that the jewelry table looks a mess and I'd like to make it nice for Daisy."

I gave her permission to do whatever she thought would make it appear more organized and she went right to it. I left her there so she could experience some creativity and feel her competence.

Rosalea had put aside a Styrofoam snowman that I had placed in the Christmas window display without any intention of selling it. I saw the sparkle in her eyes and her smile as she held it. She told Daisy that she intended to take it to her grandchildren the next day when she went to her daughter's for Christmas dinner. Daisy had told her that it was not for sale, but I whispered in her ear that if she wanted it, I would give it to her as a gift from me. I told her that I hoped that her grandchildren would enjoy it. She thanked me and I was left with feelings of gladness as well as sadness. I have a little granddaughter in Louisiana that I have not seen for two years. In fact, the only time I have seen her was the week she was born. The distance and my financial situation have made it difficult to visit her. I know that one day she will know and love her Grandy!

Betty finished sorting the jewelry and found some necklaces that she felt would be nice for Daisy, Luva Lynne and me. She held them up for us and it was evident that she was into the spirit of Christmas and gift giving. All three of us accepted the treasures that she had selected very graciously; we were certainly not going to spoil her fun. It was a silent pact amongst us. Betty decided that she would dust the kitchen items and she came down the stairs within minutes bearing a cup and saucer that she thought Daisy should have. Daisy accepted the offering with a wink at me, and I could not help but feel warmth in my heart for the girl-woman who wanted to play Santa Claus that day.

All of a sudden Betty came to the counter where Daisy and I were standing and began to recite, "The Night before Christmas" poem to us. Once again, I was moved to tears as I witnessed an innocence in her that was bringing magic to the space. Daisy picked up on her joy and they both broke out in the songs, "Jingle Bells" and then "Winter Wonderland." I am noticing as I write this that I used the words "broke out" and I can't help but feel wonder even now at the girl-child who wanted to sing out in both Daisy and Betty.

My wish is that all of us could feel that we could sing out to our hearts' content without censor from within us or outside of us. They invited me to sing with them then, and I felt a hesitation. I told Daisy that my mother always said that I had a voice like a fog horn and Daisy replied, "Well, we need a fog horn in this choir right now!" I laughed out loud and began to sing loudly!

We all had a great time; in fact, Betty was also performing

little jigs while we were singing with glee! I know that in those sacred moments of singing and dancing that we felt the Christ energy moving within us. Our sheer bliss had to be a great gift to the Creator at this special time of year.

Donald, who is Daisy's 'mountain man' because of his beard and his height, came into the store to do his two-hour weekly service. His job is to water the plants and to take the pop cans to the shed. He completed his tasks and then he took his seat on the fourth step up to the kitchen wares. He liked to engage in conversation with me when he came into the store and referred to me as the "thin lady."

He started to talk about the desire to go back to university for whatever reason. He does have a tendency to speak in streams of consciousness. He went on to say that it would be difficult for him because of the distance he would have to travel. I would never have guessed that he would have ever attended a university and he piqued my curiosity. I had experienced some of his knowledge of issues like local politics, real estate, and geography, but because of his silence at times and his tendency to ramble on at other times; I assumed that he was far more challenged than perhaps he really was. I recognized that I still had some healing to do concerning making assumptions and I was face to face with my own shadow in terms of this tendency. I felt relieved, though, that I had cultivated curiosity. I was humbled. He shared then that he had completed his first year of university in the science program but that family economics became a problem for him after that.

"What would you really enjoy doing now?" I queried.

"I would really like to play the viola," he smiled at me. "My brothers sold mine when my father passed away because they were given power of attorney over his estate. This was just before I went to the group home. I could only receive a certain amount of money per month and I could never afford one again." I noticed tears in his eyes even though he told his story with a smile.

Daisy spoke quietly to me, "It was criminal what his brothers did to Donald, and the fact that he landed in one of the worst group homes in the city was unconscionable. He would really like to move but can't at this point in time because his paper route gives him extra money, and the kind of access he needs to service his customers." Daisy was silent for a few more minutes then and added, "I would love to find him a viola. I wonder, Sandra, if you would consider putting an advertisement on Craig's list posting a need for the instrument and to direct responders to contact The Modern Services for the Handicapped. Perhaps someone would be able to donate one to us."

I answered that I would try to post one that evening. To be honest with you, I am a 'techno-peasant' in terms of computers and I wish that I had not volunteered. Garth was already furious at me for spending time at the store and writing into the night. I did not want to ask him to help me on the computer and jump-start his nightly diatribe about my focus on the store.

It was time for Daisy to have her sandwich break and she invited me once again to take my place beside her. The previous evening she had read the manuscript of a book that I had not published yet because of financial difficulties. It is titled, "Of Cats and Other Tales".

She looked directly at me and said, "Sandra, I am going to say this again. You have lived enclosed most of your life and you need to blossom." Daisy was getting so close to the bone now, and I found myself hearing her words over and over again in my mind that evening.

I was feeling captured in my home situation with Garth but was being accused that it was all in my mind. I told Garth that I felt that I was continually being set up to explain, apologize and retract especially about the way that I did my creative work. It was a 'crazy-making', and I was not sure how I was going to deal with this oppressive situation.

I was uncertain at this point in time how much my 'bad boy friend' was in my head. I certainly would not be resonating as much when things were said about my work if I was convinced of its merits myself. Obviously, I was experiencing ambivalence and unfinished business in terms of self-awareness. I certainly did not want to be interrupted in my work, but I did not get it that my focus on my work could interrupt my awareness of other needs, such as love and play, that I was neglecting. Garth was waking me up to face a shadow side of me that I was not ready to embrace. I was being stone walled by him because he was not willing to be accountable for behaviors that I felt were hurtful. I had taken on a role as standard bearer and scapegoat in a family where addiction and its ramifications had been denied and I was healing from it. When one has healed something and finds oneself in that same dynamic, the personal anxiety is a sign to stand up for what you know and feel. Self responsible assertion on my part was making things difficult for him and he had become reactive and defensive. I was on a merry-go-round called denial again and I couldn't tolerate it.

Daisy told Donald and Betty that they could leave for the day. She had pens wrapped individually with beautiful colors of string with each person's name on them. At Daisy's request, Luva Lynn had brought them back from Guatemala when she was there in the autumn. These were creative replacements for gift cards and were taped to a gift of chocolates that she chose especially for 'her people'. These two special people left the store that day with a gifting from a very special lady and I believe that they knew this in their hearts.

Luva Lynne had been in the store arranging her Guatemalan treasures for the three hours. She worked quietly as a high witness to the day's process. Before she took her leave, she hugged Daisy and me and thanked us for the high energy that she claimed to have experienced that day.

Daisy and I turned out the lights; I hugged her and walked her outside to Patty's car. We brought closure to another very interesting and pleasurable day. I did not look forward to going home and being with Garth. I was not feeling safe emotionally and I was reminded that the past was prologue to the present situation. I knew that I would have to go through the pain of confrontation and assertion. I had not been good with conflict and walking on eggshells around another is disempowering and stressful. I had already paid a high price to create an illusion of safety. I was coming to a deeper understanding for the girl I was and her pain. It would be me who had to let her off the hook so that she could feel her vibrancy again.

29

"No tears in the writer, no tears in the reader."
Robert Frost

It is Wednesday, two days before Christmas. Daisy decided to work today so that she could distribute her Christmas gifts to her workers. She usually takes Wednesdays off because she has to take her medication for osteoporosis and she needs to rest for two days. I was happy that she came in though, because I do not have a lot of alone time with her, and I need to bring this book to completion. The situation reminds me about the tale she told me about her mother who had only a few moments for her children and that could only be one at a time. "She had too many charges and obviously could only handle so much," Daisy had explained to me. Unfortunately, the child does not see things this way and usually ends up finding fault with herself.

Many people came through the door today and Daisy seemed to enjoy greeting the customers, especially the long time friends who came to wish her well. Of late, she seems to want to speak deliberately about the services that she has provided over the years through her store. She shares that she has been in this business for over thirty-seven years and that she is ninety-one years old. She speaks of helping the handicapped including the developmentally and mentally challenged, schizophrenics, the brain injured, those with bipolar depression and those who have to do community service for certain misdemeanors. Many of the women look with awe at her, and some shed tears. I am left to wonder if Daisy gives them hope for a long fulfilled life.

A man came through the door and asked me if I knew someone with the name, Donald Fisker. I did not recognize the name in the moment and directed him to speak with Daisy who was finishing with a customer.

Another customer entered and I waited on her. I was within earshot of Daisy and the man. I overheard her speak of Donald and the viola. It dawned on me then that I had not known Donald's last name. They were conversing about the "mountain man"!

This man had seen Donald in his neighborhood and knew through someone that he had met that Donald spent time at Daisy's. He had come to Daisy's to inquire about Donald because he felt drawn to help him in some way. Daisy shared the story of Donald's brothers with him and the loss of the viola. This man was a pianist. I was feeling guilty because I did not search Craig's list the night before. He offered to put an advertisement on the list that night and assured her that he would be in touch. He gave Daisy his business card and we learned that his name was Tom.

I must say that my faith in the sacredness of life was strengthened in a few moments in ordinary time during a very sacred season. We closed the store on that note.

30

> "A good story must be skillfully told: each word must count. But, more than that, a truly powerful story comes from the center of the writer's soul."
>
> *Henry Argyle*

When I entered the store today, Daisy was in tears. She took my hand in hers and said, "Sandra, something very wonderful has happened. You remember that man Tom who was in yesterday to inquire about Donald and his desire to play the viola?"

"Yes, Daisy, he was going to put an advertisement on Craig's list," I replied. How could I forget?

"Well, I got a call from him and while he was writing up the ad he decided to scan the list first. He saw a listing for a viola. Tom called the owner and went to see him. His daughter drove him out to Abbotsford because he was not familiar with the area. While visiting, Tom found out that the man had a challenged child and he and Tom came to an agreement around a very fair price for the instrument. He is bringing it to the store this very afternoon. Can you believe this, Sandra?"

"Yes, Daisy, I can! I believe that divine light is shining on us right now!" I exclaimed.

"Oh, Sandra, this is so wonderful!" I thought Daisy was about to break out into a jig.

Not long after, Tom appeared in the doorway with the viola

and its case. He pulled out the most beautiful instrument and Daisy wanted a picture taken of it. It happened to be the day that I forgot my camera. I went to find Rick to ask him to come to take a picture on his digital camera. Luckily, he answered his door. He was barefooted and had been working on a letter to his girlfriend who had gone away on holidays. I explained what had happened and he assured me that he would be right over to Daisy's.

When I returned to the store, Tom was very adamant that he not be included in the picture if it was for my book. He wanted to remain an anonymous giver. I was so inspired by this man and I assured him that the picture was for Daisy only. Rick arrived and Tom and Daisy posed for the picture holding the viola between them. This generous and humble man wanted to support one of his fellow pilgrims whose greatest desire was to experience his music again. Rick was overcome with emotions and his eyes swelled with tears.

As human beings, we are certainly both instruments and instrumental in the divine drama of life. We had all witnessed magic and mystery and how the experience of joy has much to do with the recognition of the sacred operating in life.

Tom decided that he wanted to do some shopping in the store and moved towards the Guatemalan section. Luva Lynne arrived in a most timely fashion then and Tom got busy with her inquiring about her endeavors.

Johnny entered the store with two bags in hand. One bag had pop cans that he wanted to exchange for cash and put towards the two Coca Colas that he drank the last time that he was in the store. I was feeling generous and I offered to pay for the drinks as a treat for him, but he was adamant that he had a responsibility to pay up. I have already spoken of the integrity of this young man earlier in the book. I had to honor his wishes. He opened the other bag he had toted. "See what I bought Annie, (Rick's dog) for Christmas!" He was excited. "I took some of the money that my grandpa gave me for Christmas to buy this bone and this iridescent collar." He looked so proud.

I was overcome with joy. This young man with a speech handicap who worked very hard for Daisy took the little money he received from his grandpa and bought Rick's orphan dog Annie, a gift. He was eager to take it to Rick who had returned home just minutes before Johnny arrived. Johnny had shown me the twenty-five dollar gift from his grandpa yesterday. The next time I looked out of the store window, Johnny was waving at me with Annie in tow. He had found a new friend in Annie and a source of unconditional positive regard.

Tom had witnessed all of this while he was shopping. He purchased a Guatemalan scarf for his wife and several little bags of worry dolls. Luva Lynne explained to him, "Guatemalan children made these by hand. Their belief is that if you have a worry, you must give it to the doll before you go to bed and place it under your pillow. In the morning the worry is gone."

Delaine had also come into the store to pick up some things that she had put away a few days before and also bought some Guatemalan worry dolls. Delaine often came into the store to browse. She takes care of her elderly mother, which has been a daunting task for her. She shared with me that she felt close to tears when she entered the store. Without the need to disclose her issues, she went into the clothing section where she stayed for a while and seemed to regain her equilibrium.

"When I came in today, I felt terrible and now I feel much better," she told me when she paid for her items. It continued to amaze me what some camaraderie and laughter can do for a woman.

Tom was ready to leave and I gave him the books that I had written and published. I felt grateful for his generosity towards Donald. I explained to him that "In Her Own Time" was written primarily for women and that I had had wonderful success with it in my women's groups. I explained that it also spoke to the issues of the inner feminine energies in men. He laughed and said, "My wife would tell you that I am already too identified with the feminine."

I touched his arm gently and said, "Tom, I believe that all of us, both genders, should know our masculine energies but it is becoming more and more imperative that we lead with the feminine." He smiled and shook my hand and then moved to shake Daisy's. He left saying, "This has been such a wonderful experience all around. I wish you a 'Merry Christmas' and for sure you will see me again."

It was closing time once again and Daisy and I embraced each other with a warm hug. Luva Lynne finished up in her section and the three of us stood looking at each other in a quiet state of awe. The events of the day seemed to have rendered us speechless. This was a very holy day and would be a very sacred evening. I believe that we had witnessed the true spirit of Christmas that day. The goodness expressed through Tom and Johnny, I believe, was truly Christ consciousness.

I believe that the prophet dwells in each of us. God is in the people - imminent as well as transcendent and therein lays our hope.

O Holy Night!

31

> "Of all that is written, I love only what a person hath written with his/her blood."
>
> *Friedrich Nietzsche*

When my father passed away this past year, I was thrown into what I know now was a complicated grieving. My parents had supported the myth of the sacred family system at my expense in their support of my former husband who was extremely good at manipulation. He had continued to try to control me through my parents and their connection with my children. I had made myself busy trying to prove my worth and remaining in their good graces. This never seemed to make a difference, and I was so frightened of losing the love of my children that I unconsciously sabotaged any good coming into my life. I was caught in a victim psychology and I was being humbled to the very core of my being. I had come face to face with my denial and addiction for approval that kept me disempowered. I was also being forced to see what was out of balance in my life. I had been competent in terms of achievements in the outer world like my mother who had been very gifted. Love and play was what she needed and I needed that more than anything at the time.

An intersection of primary vulnerabilities was taking place between Garth and I. I knew that relationships could be the greatest crucible for healing old wounds as they came up but both partners had to be willing to grow. I felt that Garth was projecting his unfinished business onto me and trying to fix it outside of himself. I did not want to be seen as the invalid and the one needing care as he shored up his self-esteem. I was beginning to see how he could render me 'invalidic' and circumscribed, and I did not like what was happening between us.

He was like my father in his forcefulness and tendency to shame, and I was not strong enough to take a stand. I knew more about debate than discourse. I had no idea what being cared for and protected by a man was like and there was no way I wanted to tap into the grief of not having had it. I attempted to push Garth away and was ready to run. I did just that when I decided to go to Banff and live with my daughter for a few months. I needed some time to encase myself and to make some sense out of my behaviors and anxiety. I felt suffocated and extremely anxious. I felt that I was in over my head in the water with him just as I had been with my father. I was in terrible intrapsychic pain.

I knew that I had to move into deeper knowing an unconscious something that was dark and bittersweet; I was repelled by it. I was also in constant conflict with Garth, the man/father in my outer world. The only way I could entertain the thought of going deeper into my personal truth again was that I knew that I had been there before and had come out the other side with a deeper understanding of myself. I was aware that I had to reach some insights that were there to help and to heal me. I knew that I needed to restore, transform and bind my hurt self and so; I went to Banff, the mountains and nature. I made a choice to cut myself away from the 'unilumined' self. I had to find the light in the darkness where songs of beauty could be born.

I had to come to a clearer understanding of my father within now as a complex that was still alive in me even though my dad passed away the year before. It was an organizing principle that continued to live in me, a ruling element that kept me busy doing the same things expecting different results. This part of me did not want to die and I was being drained by the 'should oughts and musts' that were continuing to drive my behavior. I was not in the driver's seat. I was not old nor was I sick. I was weary from being pulled in too many *directions. I had to become 'undone' in order not to be the way I had been any longer. I was longing for some kind of force that would help to heal me. I needed to learn to become even more connected to my authentic self so that I could release old patterns and thoughts in order to liberate myself and commit to others in relationships. I knew that one had to possess a real sense of oneself before one could give of herself authentically in a relationship. I was not ready for a relationship with a man in the outer world. I had been through a search for the Beloved of my own soul... a more loving self-supporting inner masculine.*

I also knew that I wanted to be close to my daughter for a while. I felt that I had lost her because of the divorce twenty years ago. The truth is that I had lost my relationship with the vital girl in me longer than that. The grief was underground and close to the surface now. I knew that I was' re-membering' my own inner girl in my body, mind and spirit. My body pain was stopping me from pretending and making 'nice' when I was in pain, hurt, lost, vulnerable, and with needs. She was lost to me through imposed expectations, roles and cultural proscriptions that inhibited any display of authenticity. I was lost in the woods once again but I had to humble myself and lose ego control. I was no longer anyone's therapist; I was on the operating table now needing to align myself with my true Self. I wanted and needed a balance of love, work and play. Right now, I feel the legitimacy of my writing and want to speak the truth as I have come to know it and reach a wider audience.

The predatory energy in me was no longer able to live, it had to be looked at, taken apart and used in a different way. This life sucking energy had to be transformed into becoming a self supporting energy. I could no longer look to a man in the outside world to redeem me. It was as though I had to summon my own internal Bluebeard to the parapet and strip him of his power so that I could find the inner Bridegroom and get rid of that internal bad boyfriend. I was truly in search of the Beloved of my soul. I was entering the process of being ravished by inner masculine energy and no longer ravaged. I was becoming ready to relate to another in the outside world with a true sense of my own power and authority. Garth was not that man in the outer life and he appeared in my life journey to take me deeper into myself. I had to let go of him.

While I was in Banff, I went into grief that was more complicated that I ever thought but I knew that liberation was close at hand. My daughter and son-in-law had to witness what they might have imagined looked like a mad woman coming 'undone' but I had language enough to help them to understand that all I needed was a safe holding environment. It should have been the other way around, but I was a woman of a different time. I also knew that I had to be a model of feminine development for my daughter as frightening as it might seem to her. She was in the 'hut of the Baba Yaga' now and I knew that she would survive and grow. I counted on that deep knowing. I had been following an age old pattern of self sacrifice and needing permission to live loving my own female uniqueness from my father, husband, the Holy father and God the Father. I wanted to know the feminine face of God. I could do nothing now and I wept and wept in my daughter's presence. I could not fully comprehend the 'why' and I was struggling for words. The predator within me seemed to become repelled by all of those tears and could no longer take hold of me. The absolute purity and honesty of these tears broke the power of the bad boyfriend in me. I was no longer doing so much second-guessing. I was becoming aware of my own divinity and I loved her!

I know both personally and professionally, that there was and there continues to be little emphasis given in Judeo-Christian theology or socio-culturally, to the importance of mother-daughter relationships. I was fighting the same depression that my mother had inherited from the women in her relational past. They had been suppressed and repressed by religion and politics. I did not want my daughter to inherit the pain. Mother-daughter relationships in our culture were, and still are, characterized by hatred and mutual distrust. Mothers often accept and glorify their servitude as well as sublimate their sexuality and intellect. Many continue to punish their daughters when they rebel against the old female role. I wanted to stop a legacy of pain but struggled to know how.

We are still a 'mother blaming' culture! Mommy is still safer to milk and blame than daddy. Daddy is still feared and addressed mainly in good girl tones or not addressed at all. Women mistrust and men destroy a woman who is not interested in sacrificing for someone or something. Human inequality and misery still surrounds us. Psychologically, females are trained to die and males to survive. Women are taught to go to the sacrificial altar willingly. Most women give up whatever a ghost of a vital or unique self they have when they marry and rear children. Most children in our culture invade their mother's privacy, life space, sanity and selves to such an extent that she must give up these things in order not to commit violence. Such invasion is practiced by some mothers against their children but not as frequently. Fathers invade children too. They really don't have to because they already own the entire territory and need only to make occasional forays to check their holdings. I was crossing the river of my personal and collective unconscious; I was not going to give any energy to the drowning man in the inner or outer worlds.

The 'many breasted woman' and 'our lady of prompt succor' was starting to decay in me as well. I came to recognize that my children's lives are theirs to live and my life is mine to live. I felt it all go – the guilt of the divorce, the nurturer who had gone overboard, that need to bend, propitiate, oversee and manage my children's lives to prove I had been a good mother. I had been good enough. That need to work constantly, to want them to be happy and have their world is a perfect place, jumped ship. The fear driven mother who thought it was her job to make sure that her children would not get lost and miss their destination had to be grand mothered into self responsibility. My children were responsible for their own lives and needed to take on for themselves the job of being human. I had to release myself from the burden of being 'breasts for the world' before I could take up my own life fully. I gave up the illusion of control in terms of needing to be needed to feel loveable and worthy of the good. I no longer needed permission from any one to live my life.

In spite of all my training and experience up until this threshold period in ordinary time, I had underestimated the deeply conditioned nature of a woman's compliance with literal and psychological sacrifice. This is not about blaming but accountability. The fear of economic, physical, sexual deprivation and punishment teaches a woman to value self sacrifice so highly that she quite naturally performs it. The deep unconscious resentment threatens to blow a side-wall any time. It is like trying to keep ten pounds of mud in a two pound sack. The 'good' woman turns the energy inward at herself and becomes depressed or sick. The 'tarnished angels' direct their hostility towards others and are easily provoked. She becomes the witch or the alcoholic woman who is noisier in her depression. Women talked to me in therapy more about men than their own independent identity or their relationship with other women. It is truth as I have come to know that only other women can 'make up' to each other for the lack of conscious mothering. Only women can (if they will), support the entry and re-entry of women into the human race. We need role models who can show us that if good things can happen to a woman in this male dominated culture, then there is hope for the young women and men. The young are already trying to move into a new sensibility. They are hungry for the language of spiritual development, not the language of oppression and winning at all costs. This need is manifesting in depression, anxiety, eating disorders, attention deficit disorders, rage and suicide. It is a split screen for our youth where domination and brute force is extant and insidious on the one hand, and on the other, a sensibility that is stronger than ever because of a new consciousness that is struggling to make itself known.

I realized that I went to Daisy's Treasure Trove much like I went to my grandmother's house when I was a young girl. I was safe with her and not alone, and I could write. I coped with my fears by writing myself into Daisy's story. This would help me to make the psychological journey from the old to the new. I longed to be in a happy, healthy relationship with a man, but I knew that I did not know how, because I did not love myself enough. I had not witnessed a healthy relationship between my parents who had been my template for interpersonal relating. Daisy tried to get me to realize that this dynamic was operating in me.

I felt that I had to do some growing and move into deeper self-awareness. I had to feel the pain of becoming more fully alive, without narcotizing my pain with care taking and being busy so that I do not have to feel. This was my mother complex continuing to operate in me. She took the rap as an alcoholic; she was a 'good' woman of the culture and full of resentment. She was just noisier than I was in her depression. My addiction to approval and achievements was 'nicer', and I became good at normalizing the abnormal and making nice all manner of atrocity. I was a martyr and the only saints that I knew were dead.

The shift in geography form Ontario to White Rock promoted new learning for me. I was searching for spiritual renewal when I left Ontario and I had to leave my father's house both literally and figuratively. I wanted a place in my life where my spirit could reside. I was desperate for a change to integrate into my life, to weave together the threads of my life and clearly know my values. I knew somehow, that the answer would come from a place of faith discerned from tuning into my own spiritual questions and opening up to new ways of learning.

The first job position as a therapist that I took was at what I thought would be a community relational place. Finding that place had been a longing in me for a very long time. But it became a handful of arbitrary things and practices, not at all aligned with what I believed that I came to White Rock to practice. A great deal of talk about collaborative learning often played itself out in competition there. A place can abhor the abuse of power and inequities, but on the other hand, be full of bullshit power relationships. It did not seem like the place to cast my net and to practice. My fury was a blind spot that I had to pay attention to.

While I was not certain what my work might look like, I knew, after knowing Daisy for a short time, that volunteering for her even before we discussed the book together seemed to be in alignment with what I valued. I took a leap of faith. My soul's work with her was about searching and turning inward to find my wisdom. It brought me deep questioning and guarded optimism. It rocked my core, disturbed my rhythms and required a new learning defined by private vigilance, not public affirmation. I was being pushed to authenticity and learning more about how I was acting, or reacting, in the world.

My hope at this stage of my development is that I can feel, heal, and re-connect with my true self. I want to live in a relationship, if I choose to over time, with a man who loves me, who wants to protect me, and is interested in self-awareness and in our conscious development together. I want to know the difference between care taking and care giving out of conscious choice, and to feel some control over my own life. I no longer want to draw others to me whom I can blame for controlling me or who need me to manage their equilibrium like a mother or therapist. I want to live comfortably with my own power and to be related to. I want to come home to my Self. I have decided to travel to Banff for some time out, personal relief, and introspection.

The Shift

Long ago
Yet not so long ago
she took to him
her heart a drum
beating time
an old rhythm
bringing blending
Desire wove meaning
and old laws
and father talk
wreaked havoc
with a soul
ordaining fire
and holy making

32

"I think of a writer as a river: you reflect what passes before you."

Natalia Ginzburg.

It is the New Year and the time has come for me to wrap things up in terms of the journey that I began nearly four months ago with Daisy. I moved internally and externally and lost thirteen chapters of writing while in transit to Banff. I was not sure that I could put myself through the extreme feelings provoked by writing these chapters again. Reliving some of it was painful and it was difficult to order my memories and find the language adequate to express them. It will be for you the reader to decide. I cried when I picked up my pen to write of these experiences again. I still find it difficult to imagine the courage of some of those people who blessed me with their presence. Time has carried them, as it has me, into the present. For every minute and every second that has passed, we have been struggling with the scenes left to us by loss. Daisy has kept in touch with me while I sort.

Donald comes to sit on the store stairs every Monday and plays the viola. He is finding his music again.

Rosalea comes every Tuesday to dust, enjoy Daisy, and she lives for the next time she will see her grandchildren.

Vicki continues to harass Daisy on Fridays and covets old clothes.

Neva is busy decorating a new apartment in Abbotsford and is creating a new life for herself.

Stacey takes the bus into Vancouver to work when she is not at Daisy's and waits for her mother's next singing concert.

Jane continues to go to a kind of dissociative place calmly and oddly familiar.

Winnie is undergoing chemotherapy for cancer and is struggling with the side effects.

Luva Lynne is in Guatemala seeing her friends and looking for interesting things to bring back to the store.

Ernie continues to visit Daisy frequently and to buy lottery tickets at Annie's variety store and is enjoying his new pants, belt and suspenders. He picks flowers from his garden to bring to delight Daisy and Annie.

Betty continues to work with Daisy once a week, and Daisy tells me that "Betty comes wearing jewelry enough for three women and always has her lipstick on. She asks for Rick each time she enters the store." Perhaps he has become her first crush innocently enough!

Rick goes to the Pacific Ocean everyday with his green coffee cup. He is learning, I hope, to live the questions into the answers and to struggle on his own without any back up from an idealized woman in his life. He has to wrestle that dragon before he can enter the Grail Castle. Time will tell.

I am living in Banff with my daughter and son-in-law for the time being and continue to write in a magnificent setting. I am feeling much safer and more secure within myself. I am taking an honest look at myself so that I can share more honestly with and move into more vital living: balancing love, play and work, in that order! Nature and two little dogs, Willow and Brodie have provided me with great healing in terms of required self-reflection. I walk the path to truth with them each day. My cat, Simba who survived the jaws of a coyote predator, is with me as well, and I have noticed that he is not as naive as he was when we left Ontario!

These are the ways we remain fluid like water and these are the ways of grieving.

I feel as though I had burned myself up to give light to my children – only to resign myself to be cast aside. My sole faith had been my identity as a Mother. I feel as though men had used everything beautiful about me up. My father's death this year has brought a complicated grieving and perhaps liberation at the same time. I do not understand it all yet.

There really is no ending to this book. This is only the beginning. The story never ends.

Truth has a way of finding us when we least expect it. I asked for truth, and it has revealed itself to me in the past several months. I know that I must integrate the Crone energy now and not project it outwards anymore. I had looked to Daisy to carry me across the threshold into more conscious femininity.

I have realized that I have been in a period of 'liminality', a passage from one stage of life to another. I ventured out physically, psychologically, emotionally mentally and spiritually when I left the known world of South-western Ontario. I was heeding a call to live more authentically and little did I know that I would be taken back to my past long enough so that I could move forward with joy. I had to go away to grow away so that I could come back to my Self in a different way.

I believe that I have a wisdom that comes from mistakes learned and I can Father myself. I also believe that I have come to know what it means to Mother myself by asking myself what feels most nourishing and self-enhancing from moment to moment. Isn't this is the goal of all good therapy?

I loved that Daisy survived, that her heart was intact, that her kindness was so deeply present after everything that she had endured. I want to be just like her.

The Old Woman or the Crone in me has knowledge enough to know what 'enough' is and to bring appropriate endings so that I can continue to bring new beginnings. I do believe that we find ourselves at the beginning over and over again. The wisdom gathered from having to live through to this truth helps me to become more comfortable with change. I am living into answers this very moment as I bring closure to this chapter of my life. I am a changing woman.

As much as bringing an end to my time in White Rock and my travels with Daisy Walls will bring me sadness, it becomes another of life's necessary losses. This feels much like the pain of saying good-bye to my children as they came of age and ready to leave home. I set them free, even though I had not been freed nor had the experience until lately of freeing myself. I have come 'of age' and I honor the fact that the human body knows how to age. I am entering a very spiritual and vulnerable time of my life.

My journey now is mine alone; one that I might not be able to share even with like-minded people. This is the finish line in White Rock for this long distance runner, and I hope that I leave you with lots to ponder.

When a way closes and one stage of our life is complete we are at an intersection, a Crossroads. This has been a river story for me carrying me towards possibility of a deeper purpose. Stories have a way of gathering our experiences into shapes. I am left defining my feelings and the feelings of those with whom I made connection over the course of this past year. I struggled trying to figure out where to place myself in the narrative. I had to ask, "Who am I exactly? Am I the observer? Am I a witness? Am I a critic? Am I an advocate?" I could come up with a lot of ideas having spent as much time alone over time as I have. I recognized that, essentially, I was bearing witness and facing some horrors of my past in terms of what I was dealing with in present time. There is a quiet authority that comes from direct experience.

The people that I have introduced to you in this story demonstrated the persistence of the human spirit to survive the most extreme circumstances. I believe that people need to know about their trauma and the resilience of the survivor. We need to be able to ask "What happened to you?" without turning away. I believe that we need to consider creating contexts where we can join valuing a diversity of experiences. We need to learn to bear uncertainty and open to new ways of thinking. Daisy was attempting to co-facilitate a group that belonged to her. Those that she invited in knew that they would be treated with respect, no matter what they said. If people have a chance to share their feelings and feel less isolated, their experience does not have to become distorted. The benefit that Daisy offered to the suffering was a support group that broke down their isolation.

It isn't the trauma itself that makes a person a psychiatric patient – it is the nature of the trauma when it occurs, how long it lasts, whether it is denied by others, and whether the person gets help.

When trauma is acknowledged, and the symptoms are seen as consequence, a person does not have to mistrust her own perceptions, thoughts, memories and feelings.

I now know that what I really wanted was space for myself to grieve, renew and refresh, and I have that now in Banff. The stories that we complete are only our maps. Though a woman may look scattered when she has lost touch with herself and the life she values most, what she is really doing is running about trying to recapture it. Most of the time, she is gathering information, taking a taste of different things, and grabbing at other things. She is searching for her 'real' self and does not want to 'reel 'anymore. It might be helpful if someone could tell her that but not many of us know the ways of moving into deep feminine consciousness. In the meantime, we must let her be and not judge her. As soon as she processes all of the information from the clues that she has gathered over time, she will be moving more intentionally again.

May you be as blessed as I have been with awareness, a deep sense of belonging on your journey home to self-awareness and the passion of a pure spirit.

To be continued dear pilgrims...

Epilogue

> "When you can't go forward and you can't stay where you are without killing what is deep and vital in yourself, you are on the edge of creation."
>
> *Sue Monk Kidd*

I did not expect that I would write another chapter to this book but when I gave my editor the manuscript she called soon after reading it with a very powerful statement about being affected by the writing. She suggested that I write a closing chapter to the work, and she wanted to meet Daisy. I was excited and made arrangements to meet with her at Daisy's store. They were delighted to meet one another and Daisy gifted Ann with a few treasures from her 'Treasure Trove'. Generosity begins when we see the face of another because we all want to be respected for who we are and not who we ought to be.

A Letter from the Editor:
    I met Daisy today!
    Having almost finished the initial read and edit of "A Journey with Daisy: Belonging is a Blessing", I phoned Sandra, compelled to meet Daisy and see Daisy's Treasure Trove before it was too late (read the story and you'll understand).
    Dressed in our meeting finery, my husband and I drove to the store in White Rock armed with a $5.00 bill, already conspiring to confirm that someone could actually be that perfect. Daisy was at the front counter, alone, so I bravely walked in, said "Hello", and explained that I had heard that she is the person to come and see if someone needs change for a parking meter. (Again, read the story, you'll understand).

Well, she looked at me, with a 'really?' look, turned away, and retrieved $5.00 change for me. I smiled, and introduced myself as Ann. She looked closer (remember she is 91) and said "I know you, I recognize you from the newspaper article Sandra gave me. You're helping us with the book." She continued to hold out the change, so I gently told her that we were parked okay, that I just wanted her to know that I had read the story, and was playing with her. She smiled, laughed, (she really does have the best sense of humor) and proceeded to introduce me to every person in the store.

Daisy is as delightful and generous in person as in the story, and I thank you, Sandra, for inviting me on this journey with you, and giving me the opportunity to meet and know Daisy, and you. I walked away with a couple of treasures I found on my own, a treasure that Daisy gave me as a thank you, and maybe the biggest and best treasure of all: I will be a better 'Crone' because of you and your book, Sandra, and a better person because of Daisy. Shirley set my Maiden bar, Mona set my Mother bar and I will have to strive to meet the Daisy bar!

"A Journey with Daisy: Belonging is a Blessing" is a woman's book, and if you are a woman and read it, you will get it! You can't help but be a better Maiden, Mother and Crone!

Ann Westlake, BA
Writer's Cramp Editing Consultants
Saturday, May 15, 2010

I returned to White Rock from Banff in May to complete my task of writing and publishing this book and to reunite with Daisy. I was entering a mystery once again and I was prepared to *allow it to inform me. The story of the female soul is no small thing and the hardest thing about being a writer is telling the truth. This is a story about spilled blood and I want it to carry medicine. The strength of the medicine has to do with how much one is willing to sacrifice and put into it. I want to leave deep footprints wherever I go now and*

Daisy gifted me with the story of the gift of the Muck- lucks. The old Native woman saw in Daisy what we were able to recognize in one another over time. Generosity always begins in dialogue and when one enters that space with another we offer ourselves to be changed by one another. Now, I want to assert my individual knowledge and proudly wear the battle scars of my time.

This story has been about tests of endurance and it would take me a while to absorb it. To be totally honest, I did not want to write a closing chapter. This would mean more sorting, more fear, anger, pain, questions, healing, transformation, bliss, power and freedom that come with most journeys. The story keeps unfolding as our lives are meant to unfold, evolve and that is good. It is a process that really doesn't end.

I have been sharing my journey before, during and after my crossroad or threshold experience with Daisy. I have found myself assimilating, re-reading and now settling with my Muse once again.

I have shared that I moved internally and externally. I spent time in the underground forest of my unconscious when I was with my daughter in Banff. It was itself a ritual of endurance which means to make sturdy, make robust, to strengthen and I know now that this has been the main thrust of the story. Daisy and I had been making something not just going on and on as some would think endurance means. Daisy said to me when I returned, "You and I have been on a long journey without having to travel very far." Gradually, I began to see what I had not seen before, to feel the things that I had never dared let enter my heart. I was aching literally and figuratively for the woman in me who had not yet been born.

I believe as I sit here writing now that my life story has been generative. I am grateful for all the ups and downs. I have been toughened by all of the ranging, roaming, settling, and unsettling. I recognize that I possess a very compassionate knowing now about myself and others. I am stronger and more resilient. My spirit has been strong, patient and enduring. I instinctively knew that same something in Daisy the first day that I met her. I was entering her space and the underworld of my own psyche at the same time. I would become infused with more instinctive language and knowledge and I believe as well, that I am even less understood by those who live primarily in the topside world. Most of the personal secret stories of women are the kind that family and friends are inadequate to discuss; they disbelieve or attempt to make light of them or bypass them. If they considered discussing them, these people would have to share the grief with the woman and not stand about composed. No, if they share the grief over the death of the vital woman they would have to partake in the funeral procession. They would have to weep at the grave. It would be very hard on them. She alone must consciously suffer because others will not pull together for her. Yet that inner push towards consciousness demands that her environment be cleansed of irritants and threats, and she must rid herself of anything that is oppressive. So it is only a matter of time before she musters up the courage to speak from the ground of her soul. She refuses to keep the secrets for once and for all. She allows the energy of her anger to inform her; she recognizes violation. She has something to say and believes that she is worth listening to. She no longer finds safety in being misunderstood and not noticed.

Over my lifetime, I mastered several descents and transformations that only led to my being plunged into another. I suffered loss, sacrifice, the coming of more consciousness or light following one upon another. I instinctively knew that Daisy had endured many rounds herself and there was a silent understanding between us. All of this descending and loss and finding again and strengthening are really about lifelong initiation into renewal. All women who possess deep knowing and instinct recognize the yearning for the wise old mother within. With Daisy I could share what I saw. I instinctively believed that she was trustworthy. Opening 'Pandora's Box' with her was much better than letting unresolved grief fester inside of me. She knew the difference between guilt, remorse and about the nature of grieving and the resurrection of spirit. Telling our secrets to a trusted other resurrects us from the tomb. We can grieve and grieve hard and we come out tear stained rather than shame stained. We can come out deepened fully acknowledged, and filled with new life. This is about the coming of Christ consciousness and understanding our innate female divinity. This is the process which transpired between Daisy and me.

That strong untamed part of us will hold us when we grieve because she is the instinctual self that knows how to grieve and to make noise. She can bear all the screaming, wailing, and our wishing to die without dying. That part of us will put the healing balm in the hurt places and whisper in our ears. She will feel the pain with us and not run away. There are scars from living and there are many of them but we must remember that a scar is stronger than skin. We might consider counting our years by the amount of battle scars and be proud of them.

Was it a deep longing for deepening that brought Ann, my editor, to see Daisy? Prior to her meeting with Daisy, she had shared with me, "I have to meet her, I know her and she is like another mother to me." Was she being catapulted now into the search for her internal instinctual mother?

My journey with Daisy brought me to a point in my life when I had to choose life over death in terms of unconsciously wanting to kill off parts of myself that were causing me to be ambivalent, collapsed and unable to mother myself. I had to make the adjustments of these internal mothering structures that I spoke of earlier in the book. I had to search deeply for the energy that could sustain what was unique to me. I was catapulted into descent and know now that I had made preparation over the course of my life journeys for the intensity and depth of this descent. I was in a position now of knowing that I had the strength to peer, persevere and endure. I have come to believe that a woman in her sixties is reaching a point in her life when she becomes a witness or watchwoman and puts into new form, everything that she has learned.

I returned to Daisy changed and changing. My task had been to integrate the frightened girl with the wise woman who could soothe her because I had acquired the wisdom of the older woman. Daisy had been that outer wise woman who sent me on a journey with love and trust in me to make it through and not around what I had continued to deny because of my shaky self. The journey had been restorative in that I had moved to deeper self awareness and personal responsibility. I could no longer miss my own pain and move to soothe others. It had kept me busy for most of my life but it hadn't got me anywhere. I knew when I saw Daisy again there was a radiance about her. It was as though her body had a sensing device and she had become even more beautiful. As a woman transits through the cycles of her life, her layers of defense become sheerer until her very soul begins to shine through. I could see and sense the movement of Daisy's soul in an astonishing way. I never think about Daisy's age, I see who she is.

Daisy was forced into closing the store as a result of the landowners wanting to change the structure of their building. When I arrived in White Rock she had just received the news that she had to close within the month. We were together once again mapping new psychic territory as we were bringing death to old ways of being. She handled it all with grace. Certainly, she cried many tears through the 'letting go' process and wavered with the ambivalence of her internal mother. It was her time again to find out more about the real Daisy and she refused to 'reel ' from the news regarding closure. There was grief and sorting but we were there again to face it, supporting one another in terms of deeper Self discovery. I have heard it said that disillusionment is a good thing. Daisy worried about the thirteen 'challenged' people that she had been helping and struggled with feelings of guilt for abandoning them. She learned during the week of closure of the store that few of them showed up to help her because they were no longer being funded. Rosalea and Rick were her only solid support; they were her friends. Disenchantment or disillusionment often brings a ripening and a woman's task is to re-conceive herself at this point in time. If she can give that awakening a chance, it will develop into a full blown experience that one day she will want to remember and celebrate.

While I was with Daisy, I witnessed many people come into the store to wish her well and so many of them asked her, "What will you do now?"

"I am going to learn more about Daisy," she answered with a smile. She shared that she would keep The Modern Services for the Handicapped going and plan social events in the clubhouse to maintain contact with her friends and I believe as I witnessed her process that she was not abandoning herself. I believe that it is Daisy's time to enter the stage of a woman's life when she gives less energy to saying and doing and more energy to being. There will be the slow unfolding, sometimes hidden, the always expanding nature of the process, the inevitable uneasiness, the uncertainty about the outcome, and the fearful knowing that once we bring the new consciousness forward into our lives that our lives will never be the same. There is no time line in spiritual time.

What you have read is a story about two women who came to know one another over a short time. The female spirit in each other instinctively recognized deep soul. They moved together through a stage of their lives and came to belong more to themselves in terms of authenticity and personal power. The states of being one in her self or belonging to oneself mean that belonging is truly a blessing.

The Crone in me whispers, "This is enough for now."

My hope for the reader is that you have become imprinted with a deeper knowing having read the story. We are the change that the world waits for. Go forth pilgrims and let them know that you are ALIVE! My wish for you is that you become comfortable with the Crone energy that dwells within you at all times. The heart of Crone consciousness is to become comfortable with change! Embrace the 'Changing Woman' as part of your true nature. Be assertive, intelligent, creative and capable. In the words of Nellie Mc Clung, "Never retract, never explain, never apologize – get the thing done and let them howl!" Your main source of power is to be able to speak candidly on your own behalf. You have a right to ask the hard questions and the strength to live into the answers.

One of the silliest myths that still exist about growing older is that a woman is so complete that she needs nothing and is a fountain of everything for everyone else. No! She continues as a tree or a plant that need water, air and nourishment no matter how old she becomes. The 'elder' woman is the same as a tree in that there is no finality or sudden completion. She has a beautiful root system, lovely branches and with proper care, she will continue to bear many flowers.

**Daisy Walls entered her ninety second year on September 15th, 2010.
Bless you, dearest Daisy!**

Born Again

Do not succumb Cinderella
those ashes hold no promise.
The landlady within holds
no power over the wisdom of
the Crone who sweeps clean.
The call to that black priestess
who cackles confidence
summons new authority
formerly forbidden.
This bantering camaraderie
forges a blossoming
never deemed possible.

About the Author

Sandra Colleen Johnston was a teacher of English Literature and Drama, Psychotherapist, Somatic Movement Educator and Therapist, but is now concentrating on her passion for writing. Her writing is a clever combination of prose and poetry that reflects her own voyage as it relates to the journey of the human soul.

Additional information can be found on Sandra's web site:

www.sandracjohnston.com